Advanced
Plumbing
PRO TIPS AND SIMPLE STEPS

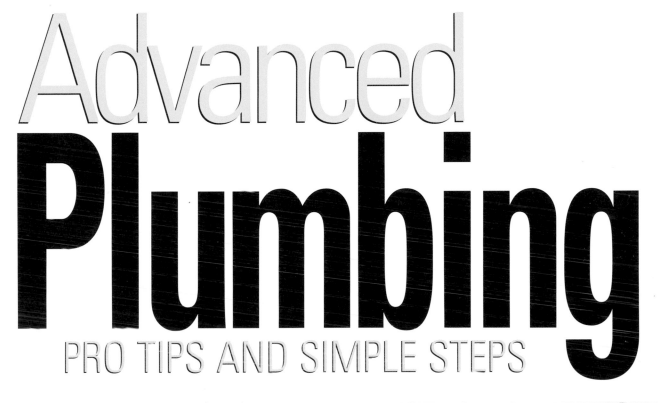

Meredith® Books
Des Moines, Iowa

Stanley® Books
An imprint of Meredith® Books

Stanley Advanced Plumbing
Editor: Ken Sidey
Senior Associate Design Director: Tom Wegner
Assistant Editor: Harijs Priekulis
Copy Chief: Terri Fredrickson
Copy and Production Editor: Victoria Forlini
Editorial Operations Manager: Karen Schirm
Managers, Book Production: Pam Kvitne,
    Marjorie J. Schenkelberg
Contributing Copy Editor: Steve Hallam
Technical Editor: Bill Rhiner
Technical Editor, The Stanley Works: Mike Maznio
Contributing Proofreaders: Kathi DiNicola, Steve Salato,
    Vicki Sidey, Jim Stepp
Electronic Production Coordinator: Paula Forest
Editorial and Design Assistants: Renee E. McAtee,
    Karen McFadden

Additional Editorial Contributions from
    Greenleaf Publishing Inc.
Publishing Director: Dave Toht
Writer: Steve Cory
Production Designer: Rebecca Anderson
Associate Designer: Jean DeVaty
Editorial Assistant: Betony Toht
Photography: Dan Stultz, Stultz Photography
Illustrator: Tony Davis
Studio Assistant: Tom Maloney
Technical Consultant: Joe Hansa, Daniel Vejr
Indexer: Nan Badgett

Meredith® Books
Publisher and Editor in Chief: James D. Blume
Design Director: Matt Strelecki
Managing Editor: Gregory H. Kayko
Executive Editor, Gardening and Home Improvement:
    Benjamin W. Allen
Executive Editor, Home Improvement: Larry Erickson

Director, Operations: George A. Susral
Director, Production: Douglas M. Johnston

Vice President and General Manager: Douglas J. Guendel

Meredith Publishing Group
President, Publishing Group: Stephen M. Lacy
Vice President-Publishing Director: Bob Mate

Meredith Corporation
Chairman and Chief Executive Officer: William T. Kerr

Chairman of the Executive Committee: E.T. Meredith III

Thanks to
B.T. Premier Plumbing, Inc.

All of us at Stanley® Books are dedicated to providing you with the information and ideas you need to enhance your home and garden. We welcome your comments and suggestions about this book. Write to us at:
    Meredith Corporation
    Stanley Books
    1716 Locust St.
    Des Moines, IA 50309–3023

If you would like more information on other Stanley products, call 1-800-STANLEY or visit us at: www.stanleyworks.com
Stanley® and the notched rectangle around the Stanley name are registered trademarks of The Stanley Works and subsidiaries.

If you would like to purchase any of our home improvement, cooking, crafts, gardening, or home decorating and design books, check wherever quality books are sold. Or visit us at: meredithbooks.com

Note to the Readers: Due to differing conditions, tools, and individual skills, Meredith Corporation assumes no responsibility for any damages, injuries suffered, or losses incurred as a result of following the information published in this book. Before beginning any project, review the instructions carefully, and if any doubts or questions remain, consult local experts or authorities. Because codes and regulations vary greatly, you should always check with authorities to ensure that your project complies with all applicable local codes and regulations. Always read and observe all of the safety precautions provided by manufacturers of any tools, equipment, or supplies, and follow all accepted safety procedures.

CONTENTS

GETTING READY

If you have successfully completed minor plumbing repairs and installations, you should be ready to move on to the more challenging work of installing new lines and adding new sinks, toilets, tubs, and showers. While a simple faucet repair spares you the time and hassle of calling in a pro, installing plumbing for a new bathroom saves a sizeable chunk of cash.

Gaining understanding and skills

This chapter shows how plumbing systems in general work and teaches you in particular how to map your house's plumbing. Armed with this knowledge, you can plan how to tap into old pipes and run new lines. It is especially important to work closely with a local plumbing inspector.

Chapter Two shows you how to plan, cut, and join all types of pipes. With an hour or two of practice, you will be able to make professional-quality joints.

Replacements and repairs

In Chapter Three you'll learn how to remove and and replace a bathtub and shower. Chapter Four helps you tackle several projects that homeowners typically shy away from, including repairing and replacing a water heater, installing a water filter, and clearing drain lines. Step-by-step instructions bring these tasks within the reach of any do-it-yourselfer.

Running new service

Chapters Five and Six focus on specific projects—a new bathroom and a new kitchen—that call for running new pipes as well as installing new fixtures. A new installation requires drawing a plan that satisfies local plumbing codes; it also requires some carpentry skills. Care must be taken not to compromise the house's structural integrity when making way for new drainpipes and supply lines, whether plumbing is installed in a new addition or in existing walls and floors.

Before tackling a project, understand plumbing in general and your system in particular.

CHAPTER PREVIEW

Shutting off water
page 6

Hiring a pro
page 7

Understanding the systems
page 8

Principles of venting
page 10

Consider using separate buckets for different categories of tools. One bucket can hold general carpentry tools, while another holds tools for cutting and joining pipe.

Because most of a plumbing system is behind walls and ceilings, demolition is one of several carpentry skills needed in a plumbing project. Allow plenty of working space when opening up a wall—making a large patch takes slightly more time than a small patch.

Plumbing tools
page 12

Pipes
page 16

Pipe fittings
page 18

Mapping a home plumbing system
page 20

Plumbing codes
page 22

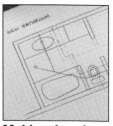

Making drawings
page 26

SHUTTING OFF WATER

All adult and teenage members of a household should know how to shut off water in a plumbing emergency. And for most plumbing projects, the first step is to turn off the water, either to a specific fixture or to the entire house.

Finding shutoffs

In most homes, there are four possible ways to shut off water. Every faucet, tub, shower, and any other fixture should have **stop valves,** often called fixture shutoffs, for both hot and cold water supplies. If you have an older home without stop valves, you'll have to shut off water to part or all of the house before repairing or replacing a fixture. To ease future repairs, install stop valves while the water is shut off.

   Intermediate shutoff valves control water flow to one or two rooms. Usually there are two ways to turn off water to an entire house: a **house shutoff valve** and a **utility shutoff,** often located underground between the house and the street.

   If the shutoff or stop valve is a globe type, turn it clockwise until you feel it stop. Most gate valves shut off in the same way, but a few have a pivot-type gate. You can turn and turn such a valve and it will not stop. Have a helper watch the water as you turn the valve slowly; each quarter turn will turn the water off or on. The handle of a ball-type valve moves a quarter turn in either direction but stops when fully on or off.

Making sure the water is off

After turning off a stop or shutoff valve, open the faucet you will be working on or flush the toilet. If the fixture has a stop valve, the water will stop immediately (a toilet will flush but the tank won't refill). If you have turned off an intermediate or house shutoff, it may take a while for the pipes to empty, especially if the fixture is on the first floor of a multistory house.

   An older shutoff or stop valve may not seal completely and will drip even after the valve is turned off. In this case, shut off water to the whole house. If water still drips, slightly open a faucet that is at a lower point than the one you are working on; the water will drip there instead.

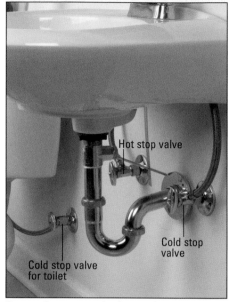

Stop valves—one for hot and one for cold water—are typically found directly below a sink faucet. A single, cold-water stop valve should be located near a toilet. The stop valves for a tub or shower faucet may be located behind an access panel *(page 24)* in an adjoining room, or they may be integral to the faucet.

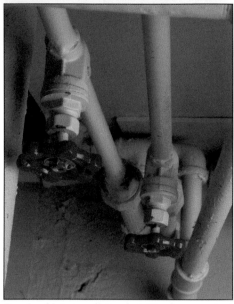

A pair of intermediate shutoff valves control water flow to one or two rooms. Shut them off and test to find out which rooms they control.

A house shutoff valve may be located near the water meter (if there is one) in a basement, in a crawlspace, or at the point where water first enters the house. In an area with a warm climate, it may be on the outside of the house.

The utility shutoff valve is typically located in an underground enclosure sometimes called a Buffalo box. The utility company may require that it shut off the water, using a special "key." In some cases, a standard shutoff handle may be within reach.

HIRING A PRO

There are many reasons to hire a pro rather than doing a job yourself: Local codes may require that only licensed contractors perform certain types of work. Some types of work call for the expertise of a qualified plumbing contractor. And even if you are competent to do the work, you may not have the time. Rather than forcing your family to live in a work site for months, it may be worth the extra money to hire someone who can get the job done quickly.

Choosing a plumber
For a major job, obtain quotes from two or three plumbers. Ask for references and talk to former customers to see whether they were satisfied. Make sure the plumbing contractor is licensed and bonded to work in your area and has liability and worker's compensation insurance so you will be protected in case of an accident.

Levels of plumber involvement
Most professional plumbers would rather do all the work themselves. However, if you feel confident that you can work on a project and need only a bit of reassurance that you're installing things correctly, a plumber may agree to work as a consultant. Often an hour spent with a pro can save you plenty in materials and labor.

You might hire a plumber to do only the "rough-in" work of running supply and DWV (drain-waste-vent) pipes. Once the rough plumbing is installed, have a local inspector approve it before you finish paying the plumber. Then you can close up the walls and install the fixtures.

Working with a plumber
Once the work has begun, use this book to see how the job ought to be done. If you are dissatisfied, or if you do not understand what the plumber is doing, don't hesitate to ask questions.

Be firm but polite. Whenever possible, save all your questions for the end of the day, so you won't be a nuisance. However, if you feel the work is shoddy or the plumber is shrugging off your concerns, make it clear that you will not pay until you are satisfied. Have all work inspected.

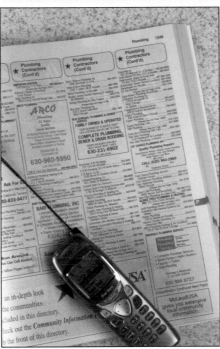

Finding a quality plumbing contractor begins with a phone call, but requires follow-up with references, assurance of proper licensing and insurance, and a clear understanding of what, how, and when the work will be performed.

What to look for in a contract

A professional plumber should have a standard contract that covers the following items:
■ The plumber's license, bonding, and insurance company should be on the form. Make sure you are absolved of responsibility in case of accident.
■ A list that clearly specifies all materials. Check the brand names and models of appliances and fixtures to make sure a cheaper model will not be installed.
■ The plumber should be responsible for pulling the permits and meeting the inspector for all inspections.
■ A timetable should clearly state when the work will be finished. To be sure work is done in a timely manner, there should be a substantial penalty for late work.
■ Payments should come at no less than three points. Up-front money should be less than half. Payments during the course of the job should occur when specified work is completed and approved by the inspector. The final payment, to be paid only when you are completely satisfied, should be substantial enough to motivate the plumber to finish.

SAFETY FIRST

Most plumbing projects do not put you in harm's way. However, use common sense and take precautions to protect yourself and your home.
■ For most jobs, rule No. 1 is: Shut off the water, then run water until it stops to make sure it has been shut off.
■ If a job will cause you to get wet, keep away from any live electrical receptacles or fixtures. To be sure, first shut off the power at the service panel.
■ Be sure you know which pipes are which. In addition to plumbing pipes, your home may have gas pipes and pipes that carry hot water for the heating system.
■ When working with or near gas pipes, shut off the gas at a point prior to where you are working and open doors or windows to provide ventilation. Do not ignite any sparks or flames and avoid touching electrical devices.
■ Drain lines may contain gases that not only smell bad but also are hazardous. Keep the area well ventilated and wear protective eyewear and clothing.
■ If at any point you are unsure of what you are doing, stop work. Consult this book and other resources until you gain confidence. Or call in a professional for advice.
■ When soldering copper pipe, protect all flammable surfaces that may be touched by the flame. Keep a fire extinguisher on hand.
■ Use the tool that's designed for the job.
■ Take the time to make the work site comfortable. Spread towels as cushions and illuminate the area with a stand-up flashlight.

UNDERSTANDING THE SYSTEMS

The maze of pipes running through your walls and floors involve two basic systems; the supply system, which brings water into the house, and the drain-waste-vent system, which carries wastewater and gases out of the house.

Supply system

In a typical system, a single **supply pipe,** ¾-inch to 1¼-inch inside diameter, brings water into the house. This water is supplied by a utility company, which is responsible for its purity.

Soon after entering the house, most supply pipes run through a **water meter,** which records for billing purposes the amount of water you use. If your water bill is the same from month to month, your water is probably unmetered.

The supply pipe then travels toward the **water heater.** There the pipe splits into two branches. One supplies cold water to the house and the other fills the water heater. The pipe that emerges from the water heater supplies hot water to the house.

Pipes branch out and run in pairs to supply hot and cold water to various rooms. Vertical pipes are sometimes called risers.

Older supply pipes are typically made of galvanized steel, while newer homes have pipes made of copper or plastic PVC or CPVC. (See *pages 16–17* for the characteristics of each.)

Somewhere near the water heater, pipes usually reduce in size to ¾ inch. Farther on, as they turn into branch lines, pipes typically reduce to ½ inch. If water pressure is low, the problem may be supply pipes that are not large enough or calcium buildup.

The flow of water can be shut off before the water enters the house, at a **main shutoff** just inside the house, at branch lines, and near the individual plumbing appliances (see *page 6*).

Drain-waste-vent system

Carrying water out of a house smoothly is the job of the DWV (drain-waste-vent) pipes. These pipes must be installed according to precise specifications of complex plumbing codes. Never install a DWV pipe until you are sure you comply with local codes.

Drain water for every fixture must run through a **trap** made of plastic or chromed brass that is thinner than house pipe and is easily dismantled. A trap is shaped like a sideways P or an S. This shape traps water so fumes and gases cannot back up into the house. A toilet has its own built-in trap.

A trap usually connects to a **branch drainpipe,** typically 1½ inches or 2 inches in diameter. A branch drain carries water to the main stack.

Drainpipes must be correctly sloped so that water can run freely through them. Special fittings that make sweeping rather than abrupt turns *(page 19)* are required by plumbing codes so that waste matter does not get stuck.

The centerpiece of a DWV system is the **main stack,** a fat pipe usually 4 to 6 inches in diameter, which runs straight up through the roof. Often a home has one or more **secondary stacks,** perhaps 2 or 3 inches in diameter that serve the kitchen or another part of the system.

Older homes have stacks made of cast iron, while newer homes use plastic ABS or PVC pipe. (See *pages 16–17* for the characteristics of each.)

Drain lines and stacks often have cleanouts, which are places where a plug can be temporarily removed to allow a clog to be augered out.

The drain for every fixture must be connected in some way to a **vent pipe,** which usually extends up through the roof. In the most common arrangement, a stack extends upward so that its upper portion acts as a vent while its lower portion is a drain. Sometimes a separate pipe is used for a vent. A **revent** reaches up and over its appliance to tie into a stack.

Vent pipes need not be as large as drainpipes, but they must be kept clear. A vent may become clogged by a bird's nest or the debris from reroofing. If so, be sure to clear it out with an auger.

Venting keeps water flowing smoothly (see below left) and also carries noxious fumes out of the house. Whenever you install new service, it is very important to have the venting installed and operating correctly (see *page 10*).

Fluid dynamics

To illustrate why venting is needed, an overturned bottle with a narrow mouth *(left)* will gurgle and glug as water pours out. The same would happen with a gas can (right) were it not for the little vent hole, which allows air to enter behind the flowing liquid, producing a smooth, steady flow.

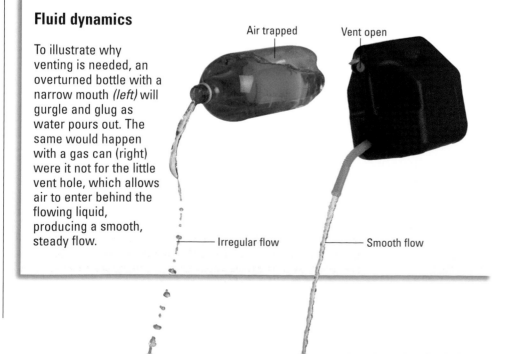

Air trapped

Vent open

Irregular flow

Smooth flow

HOUSEHOLD SUPPLY LINES, VENTS, AND DRAINS

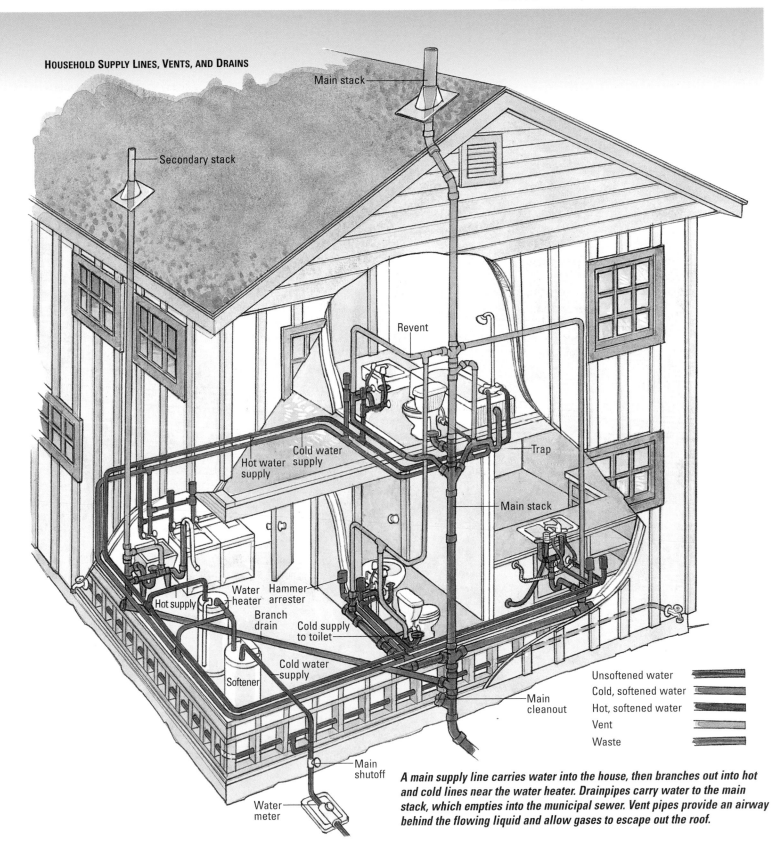

Main stack

Secondary stack

Revent

Cold water supply

Hot water supply

Trap

Main stack

Hot supply

Water heater

Hammer arrester

Branch drain

Cold supply to toilet

Softener

Cold water supply

Main cleanout

Main shutoff

Water meter

Unsoftened water	
Cold, softened water	
Hot, softened water	
Vent	
Waste	

A main supply line carries water into the house, then branches out into hot and cold lines near the water heater. Drainpipes carry water to the main stack, which empties into the municipal sewer. Vent pipes provide an airway behind the flowing liquid and allow gases to escape out the roof.

PRINCIPLES OF VENTING

How will the drain be vented? That's the first question that must be answered as you plan for plumbing a new appliance or an addition to your system. When developing a plumbing system plan, you may have the option to choose from several venting types; keep in mind that each option may present its own problem or complication. Before finalizing a plan, have the venting scheme approved by the local plumbing inspector.

Vent Types

A **true vent** is a vertical pipe attached to a drain line that runs up through the roof with no water running through it. If a fixture is close to the stack and is on the top floor,

the upper part of the stack serves nicely as a vent (as is the case for the toilet shown below). However, many fixtures are not so conveniently located and other solutions must be found.

A **revent** pipe, also called an auxiliary vent, attaches to the drain line near the fixture and runs up and over to the main vent. It may attach directly behind the fixture (sink, below) or to the horizontal drain line (revent alternative, opposite).

If two fixtures are on opposite sides of a wall, they may tie into the stack with a sanitary cross; this is called a **common vent** (back-to-back sinks, opposite).

When a fixture is close enough to a stack, a wet vent (tub, below) may be allowed by

code. In this case the tub's drain empties into a pipe through which water flows.

If a sink is freestanding in the middle of a room, a **loop vent** (opposite) may be allowed by code.

If reventing is difficult and wet-venting is not allowed, it may be necessary to install a separate vent. This requires running a separate vent pipe through the roof (see *page 89*).

The "critical distance"

Can you install a wet vent, or do you have to install a revent or a separate vent? Finding the answer can involve fairly complicated calculations, based on formulas that can

TYPICAL VENTING ALTERNATIVES

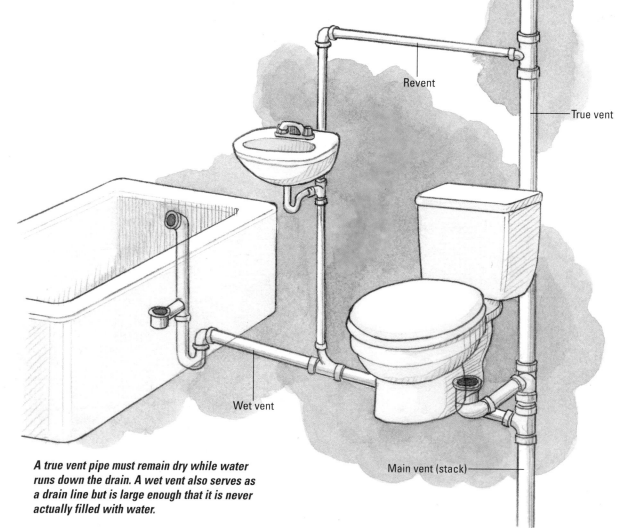

Revent

True vent

Wet vent

Main vent (stack)

A true vent pipe must remain dry while water runs down the drain. A wet vent also serves as a drain line but is large enough that it is never actually filled with water.

vary from one building department to another. The size of the vent pipe, the type of fixture, and the number of fixtures that are already wet-vented into the pipe are three factors that determine the "critical distance"—how far the fixture can be from the vent pipe. Measure the pipes carefully and consult with a plumbing inspector to determine whether wet-venting is possible.

Installing vent pipes
Vent pipes are often smaller in diameter than the drainpipes they serve. They need not slope like drainpipes. Normally they run either level or plumb, unless there is an obstacle.

Vent pipes must be installed so that they stay dry when water runs through the drain line. That means that they should emerge from the top of the drainpipe, either straight vertically or at no less than a 45-degree angle from horizontal, so that water cannot back up into the vent.

The horizontal portion of a revent pipe must be at least 6 inches above the fixture's "flood level"—the highest point to which water can rise. (On a sink, the flood level is the sink rim or overflow hole.)

The main drain
Plan drain lines to minimize the possibility of clogs. The general rule is that smaller

pipes—1¼ inch for bathroom sinks and 1½ inch for kitchen sinks, for instance—lead to larger branch drains. These in turn lead to the main stack, which is the largest pipe of all—typically 4 inches. Besides being large, the main stack is vertical, so it will rarely clog.

The main stack leads down into the ground and then out toward the municipal sewer. The underground horizontal pipe, or main drain, that runs toward the sewer line can sometimes get clogged, especially if it is an old drain made of clay pipe. (For how to clear a clogged main, see *pages 74–75*).

OTHER VENTING OPTIONS

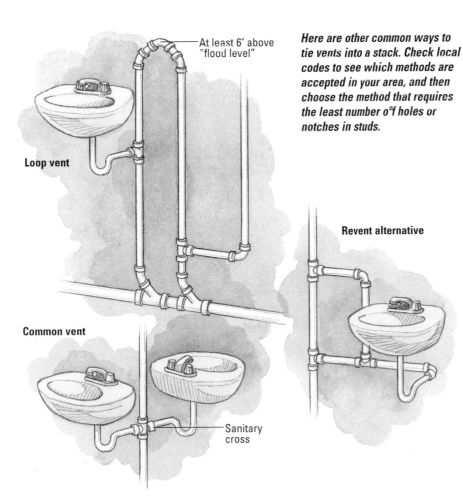

At least 6" above "flood level"

Loop vent

Common vent

Sanitary cross

Here are other common ways to tie vents into a stack. Check local codes to see which methods are accepted in your area, and then choose the method that requires the least number of holes or notches in studs.

Revent alternative

Catch basin

Many people pour grease down a kitchen sink. In time, this can lead to clogged drain lines. In some older homes, the kitchen sink has its own stack, and the drain line runs out to a catch basin—a container that traps grease. Occasionally the grease must be removed from the catch basin. A catch basin typically is located behind the house and has a large metal cover. In many cases, however, the catch basin has been bypassed and is no longer in use. There may also be a rectangular grease trap under the kitchen sink. This needs to be cleaned regularly.

PLUMBING TOOLS

For a modest amount of money—probably less than a single visit from a plumber—you can assemble a tool kit that will tackle most jobs in your house. Invest in quality tools. They will stand up to tough tasks and be more comfortable to use.

General plumbing tools
These tools are useful no matter what material your pipes are made of. You'll need both **phillips** and **slot screwdrivers** to disassemble fixtures and fittings. An **adjustable wrench** adjusts to grab nuts

and bolts. A pair of **groove-joint pliers** is useful for tightening and loosening all sorts of joints. A **14-inch pipe wrench** is the ideal size for most projects. (To add to its persuasive force, slip a 1¼-inch steel pipe over the handle to increase the leverage.) If you will be working on steel pipe, buy a pair of pipe wrenches (add an 18-inch size).

To clear clogs in sinks, toilets, and tubs, first try a **flanged plunger,** whose funnel-like flange extends to fit snugly into a toilet. To plunge a sink or tub, fold up the flange. If the clog is in a sink trap, you can often

pull the hair and gunk out with a **ribbed plastic declogger.** When these measures do not clear a clog, use a **hand-crank auger,** also called a snake. A **toilet auger** fits into the toilet and has a sleeve to protect the toilet bowl's porcelain finish.

A **basin wrench** reaches into small spaces to loosen or tighten hold-down nuts. Without this tool, removing a kitchen or bathroom faucet is nearly impossible. To remove a large nut like that beneath a kitchen sink basket strainer, a **lock-nut wrench** is easier to use than groove-joint pliers. When

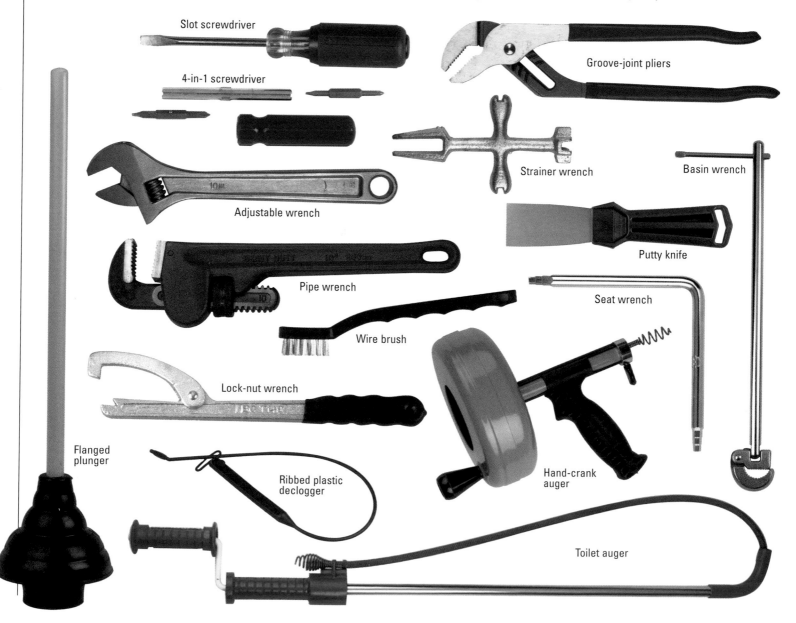

Slot screwdriver

Groove-joint pliers

4-in-1 screwdriver

Strainer wrench

Basin wrench

Adjustable wrench

Putty knife

Pipe wrench

Seat wrench

Wire brush

Lock-nut wrench

Hand-crank auger

Flanged plunger

Ribbed plastic declogger

Toilet auger

repairing a faucet, you may need to get at the seat, a small part located inside the faucet body. Use a **seat wrench.** A **strainer wrench** helps you twist out the upper part of the drain assembly in a sink or tub.

Use a **wire brush** to clean parts and encrusted pipe threads. A **putty knife** scrapes away old putty and other types of hardened debris. A **hacksaw** is useful for cutting steel and copper pipes and for removing rusted fittings. Have a **close-work hacksaw** for working in tight areas.

A **right-angle drill** makes it possible to drill straight holes in tight places—handy when running pipe.

Tools for plastic pipe

You can use just about any saw to cut plastic pipe—a hacksaw, a standard backsaw, an ordinary handsaw, a circular saw, or even a table saw. However, an inexpensive **plastic pipe saw** (also known as a PVC saw) cuts easily and leaves few burrs to remove. Use it along with a **miter box** to ensure straight cuts. For large

projects a **power miter box** (or chopsaw) with a fine-cutting blade makes even quicker and neater cuts.

To cut supply pipe (1 inch and smaller), you can also use a scissors-type **plastic pipe cutter.** Be sure to get a heavy-duty model made for PVC pipe. For PEX and other flexible tubing, a **plastic tubing cutter** makes a quick, clean cut. After cutting, burrs must be removed completely, or it will be difficult to slide on fittings. A utility knife works, but a special **deburring tool** does the job better and more quickly.

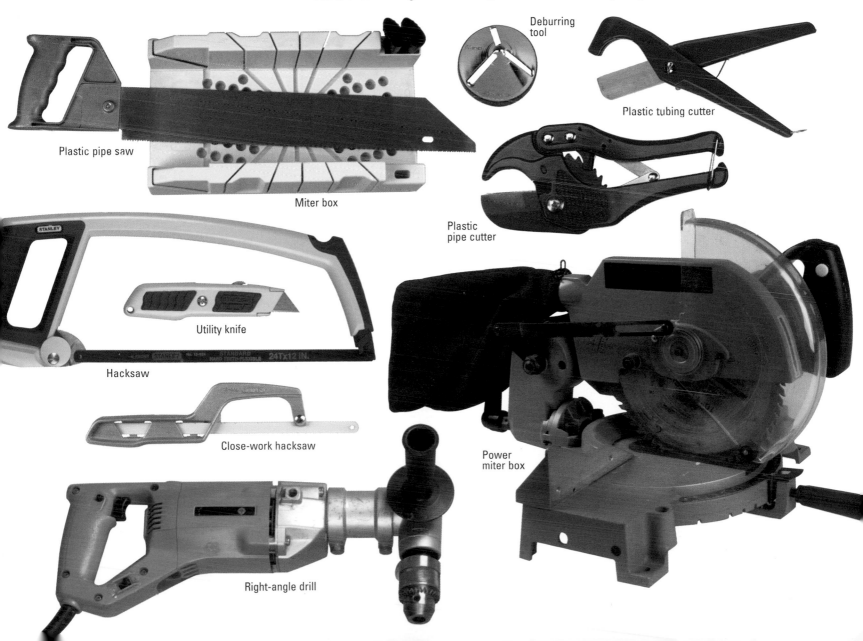

Plastic pipe saw

Miter box

Deburring tool

Plastic tubing cutter

Plastic pipe cutter

Hacksaw

Utility knife

Close-work hacksaw

Power miter box

Right-angle drill

PLUMBING TOOLS *(continued)*

Tools for copper pipe

A **tubing cutter** cuts copper pipe cleanly, quickly, and without bending the pipe out of round. For working in tight spots, you might need a **small tubing cutter** as well. (A hacksaw can cut copper pipe; but a dull blade may cause you to dent the pipe, making it very difficult to add fittings.)

For bending flexible pipe without crimping, use a **tubing bender.** Choose the size that just slips onto the pipe. A **flaring tool** may be needed for certain types of compression fittings, particularly in outdoor installations.

To sweat copper pipe and fittings, buy a **propane torch.** A model with an electric igniter is easiest—and safest—to use. To protect flammable surfaces from the propane torch's flame, use a **fiber shield** or prop an old cookie sheet behind the joint being heated.

The ends of copper pipe and the insides of fittings must be burnished before soldering. A **multiuse wire brush** does both jobs. Or buy a **reamer brush** for the fittings and a roll of **plumber's emery cloth** for the pipe ends. Before joining pipes, paint **flux**

on the pipes using a **flux brush.** A **stand-up flashlight** makes it easier to work in cramped, dark quarters.

Remodeling tools

When running new plumbing lines, much of your time will be spent cutting and drilling to clear a path for the pipes. This work must be done with a fair amount of precision so that the house's framing will not be compromised. Good tools help. So in addition to plumbing tools, have on hand a set of general carpentry tools, including a

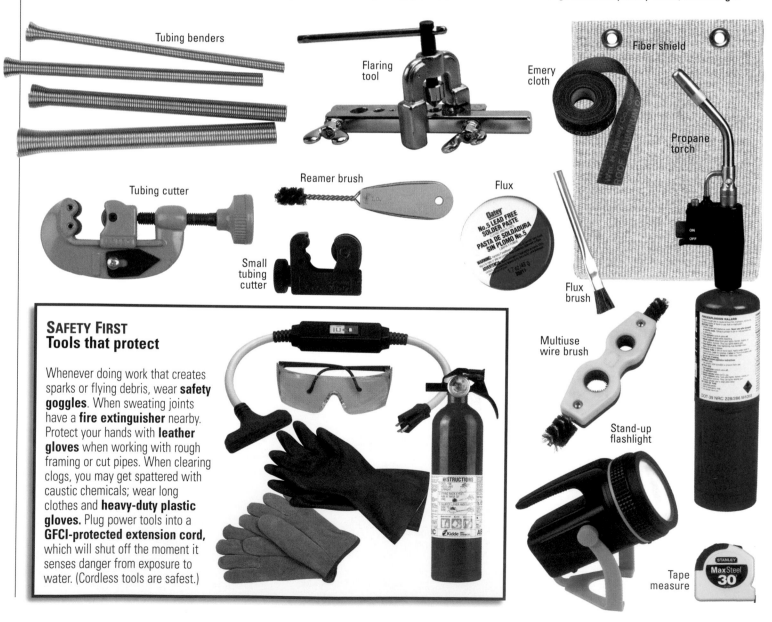

Tubing benders

Flaring tool

Fiber shield

Emery cloth

Propane torch

Tubing cutter

Reamer brush

Flux

Small tubing cutter

Flux brush

Multiuse wire brush

Stand-up flashlight

Tape measure

SAFETY FIRST
Tools that protect

Whenever doing work that creates sparks or flying debris, wear **safety goggles**. When sweating joints have a **fire extinguisher** nearby. Protect your hands with **leather gloves** when working with rough framing or cut pipes. When clearing clogs, you may get spattered with caustic chemicals; wear long clothes and **heavy-duty plastic gloves.** Plug power tools into a **GFCI-protected extension cord,** which will shut off the moment it senses danger from exposure to water. (Cordless tools are safest.)

hammer and **tape measure**. A **flat pry bar** will enable you to disassemble most nailed-together framing members. Occasionally you may need a longer pry bar. Demolition chores may require small or large sledge hammers.

Should your project call for cutting through subflooring or notching framing members, a **reciprocating saw** is indispensible. It reaches in to cut boards in tight and awkward spots and can even slice through nails and screws. You can also use it to cut into galvanized steel drain and supply lines. Buy a variety of blades for it, including metal-cutting blades.

To get to pipes inside a wall, you'll need to cut through drywall or plaster. Use a **drywall saw** or a **jigsaw**. Use a **circular saw** for notching studs and, with a metal-cutting blade, for cutting cast-iron pipe.

Use a **standard ³⁄₈-inch drill** to bore holes in 2× lumber. If you have to drill more than 10 holes, consider renting or buying a heavy-duty, ¹⁄₂-inch drill. Regular spade bits will wear out quickly, so buy several or invest in an auger bit. Attach spade bits to a **bit extender** when extra reach is needed. Make finder holes with a **long bit**. For cutting holes larger than 1 inch in diameter, you'll need a **hole saw**.

If you need to cut away a small amount of concrete or masonry, a hammer and **cold chisel** may be all you need. To chisel out a large area, rent an **electric jackhammer**, also known as a chipper.

Horizontal drainpipes must slope slightly. To check the slope, use a **carpenter's level** for long sections of pipe and a **torpedo level** for short sections.

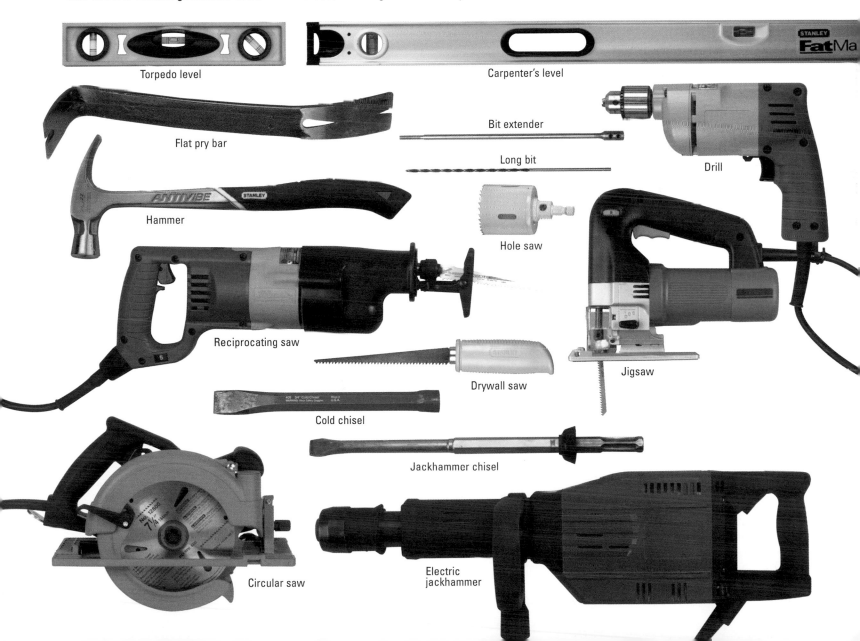

Torpedo level

Carpenter's level

Flat pry bar

Bit extender

Long bit

Drill

Hammer

Hole saw

Reciprocating saw

Jigsaw

Drywall saw

Cold chisel

Jackhammer chisel

Circular saw

Electric jackhammer

PIPES

The new pipes you install will probably be either copper supplies or PVC drainpipes. However, it's also likely that you'll encounter other types of pipe, such as galvanized steel and even cast-iron. If you have only a short run to make, you may choose the original material type. However, most inspectors would prefer that you use copper or PVC, which are less expensive and easier to install.

Cast iron

Most homes built before the 1960s have cast-iron vertical stacks and perhaps cast-iron horizontal drainpipes as well. This material is strong and usually durable; a pipe in good condition can be expected to last for decades. However, it can rust. It's not unusual for one or two sections to rust through while the rest of the pipe remains in good shape. Sections of cast-iron pipe can

be replaced using plastic pipe with transition fittings.

In older cast-iron installations, each pipe has a bell-shaped "hub" at one end *(below)* into which the next pipe's straight end fits. The joint is sealed by packing it with oakum—a kind of oily fiber—and then pouring in molten lead. Newer cast-iron pipe is joined with "no-hub" fittings, comprised of neoprene sleeves tightened with stainless-steel clamps.

Plastic

Plastic pipe is inexpensive and easy to use. Joints are glued together using primer and cement made for the particular type of plastic *(pages 32–33)*.

Black **ABS** (acrylonitrile-butadiene-styrene) pipe was the first plastic pipe to be used in homes. It is no longer permitted in

many areas because its joints occasionally come loose, but normally it can be expected to last. (For how to install or add on to ABS, see *pages 33 and 42.)*

White or cream-colored **PVC** (polyvinyl-chloride) pipe is now the most common choice for drainpipes. It lasts nearly forever, is strong, and is impervious to most chemicals. Stamped printing on the pipe tells the pipe size, as well as its "schedule," an indication of strength. Schedule 40 is considered strong enough for most residential drain lines.

Schedule 80 PVC is sometimes used for cold-water supply lines, though many inspectors disapprove of it. It definitely should not be used for hot-water supply, because it shrinks and expands with changing temperature. **CPVC** (chlorinated polyvinyl-chloride) pipe has the strength

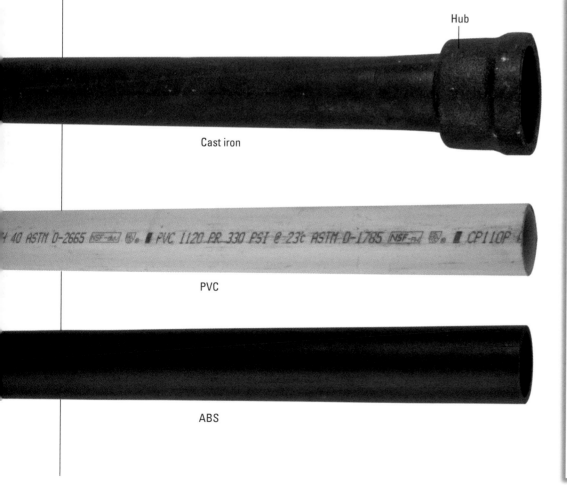

Hub

Cast iron

PVC

ABS

Pipe sizes

Material	Outside Circumference	Inside Diameter
Copper		
	2"	½"
	2¾"	¾"
	3½"	1"
Steel (galvanized or black)		
	2"	⅜"
	2⅜"	½"
	3⅛"	¾"
	4"	1"
	4¾"	1¼"
	5½"	1½"
	7"	2"
Plastic (PVC, CPVC, or ABS)		
	2¾"	½"
	3½"	¾"
	4¼"	1"
	5⅛"	1¼"
	6"	1½"
	7½"	2"
	10½"	3"
	14"	4"
Cast Iron		
	7"	2"
	10⅛"	3"
	13⅜"	4"

of PVC and is also heat resistant, so many codes allow its use for interior supply lines *(pages 34–35).*

New **PEX** supply pipe has a hoselike flexibility and joins with compression fittings, making it very easy to install *(page 35)*. However, it is expensive and is not allowed by many codes.

Steel pipe

Many older homes have **galvanized steel** pipe for supply lines, and possibly for branch drain lines as well. It is a dull gray when old and slightly shiny when new.

Galvanized pipe is strong—it's very difficult to drive a nail through it—but don't expect it to last more than 50 years. Joints develop rust and, even worse, the insides can become clogged with mineral deposits, causing low water pressure.

Black steel pipe is used for gas lines only. It should not be used for water supply because it rusts more quickly than galvanized steel. (An exception: In some areas black steel is used for water supply lines leading into a boiler, steam lines, and air lines.)

Steel pipe is joined to fittings by first wrapping the threads with pipe-thread tape or covering them with pipe joint compound (which may be either gray or white) and then tightening. The joints must be very tight; inadequately tightened joints may eventually leak.

Copper

Copper pipe is extremely long lasting and resists corrosion, making it ideal for supply pipes. It is more expensive than plastic but still reasonably priced.

Rigid copper pipe comes in three thicknesses: The thinnest, rated "M," is usually considered strong enough for most residential purposes. Thicker pipes, rated "L" or "K," are used outdoors and for drains.

Rigid copper pipe is joined to fittings by "sweating"—soldering the pieces together. A well-soldered joint should be wiped smooth; if there is a visible drip, the joint may not be strong *(pages 30–31).*

Flexible copper tubing is often used to supply an icemaker, dishwasher, or other appliance. It is easily bent to make fairly tight turns. If it gets kinked, however, there's no way to fix it; the piece must be replaced. It is joined to fittings and valves using compression fittings *(page 106)* or soldered.

STANLEY PRO TIP

Finding the inside diameter

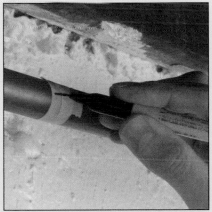

To find out a pipe's "ID"—inside diameter—first wrap a piece of tape or a strip of paper around the pipe, then make a mark to indicate the outside circumference of the pipe. Then use the Pipe Sizes chart *opposite* to find the inside diameter of the pipe.

1/2" BRISTOLPIPE PVC 1120 SCH 40 ASTM D-1785 CPVC

CPVC

PEX tubing

Galvanized steel

Black steel gas pipe

Rigid copper

Flexible copper tubing

PIPE FITTINGS

Whatever the material, most fittings fall into four categories: couplings, which join pipes in a straight line; elbows, which turn corners; tees, Ys, and crosses, which allow pipes to branch out into new lines; and caps, which seal the ends of pipes.

Always buy more fittings than you think you need—they're cheap, and people tend to undercount while planning.

Supply fittings

Copper, threaded steel, and plastic supply elbows (also called ells) are available in 90- and 45-degree angles. A **standard elbow** has two female openings of the same size; a **reducer elbow** has one opening that is smaller. A **street elbow** has one female and one male end and is useful in tight spots. A brass **drop-ear elbow**, or **stubout**, has two wings which can be screwed tightly against a wall. Some can be sweated; some have threaded ends.

A **straight tee** fitting has three openings all the same size. A **reducer tee** has one smaller opening to accommodate a smaller pipe. Usually the two openings opposite each other are larger, and the perpendicular one is smaller.

Couplings simply join pipes in a straight line. A copper or plastic slip coupling, also known as a repair coupling, can slide all the way onto one pipe, allowing you to join two pipes that are rigidly held in place and cannot be moved to the side. A **reducer** **coupling** makes a transition to a smaller pipe size.

Threaded steel pipe (both galvanized and black gas pipe) can be assembled moving in one direction only because all the threads are clockwise. To break into a line, use a special coupling called a **union,** which has three parts; it allows you to dismantle and join pipes from either side.

When changing pipe material, be sure to use the correct transition fitting. Use a dielectric fitting *(page 36)* when joining copper to steel. It has a plastic seal that stops the ionization process that would otherwise corrode the joint. Plastic-to-steel and plastic-to-copper transition fittings are also available.

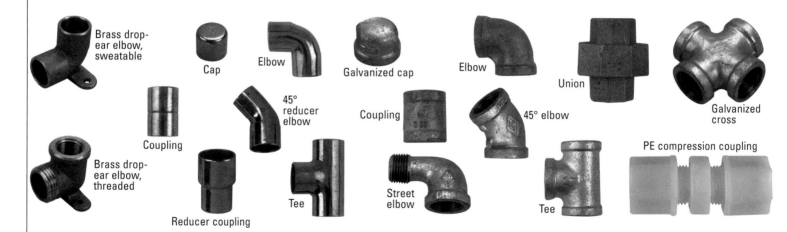

Brass drop-ear elbow, sweatable

Cap

Elbow

Galvanized cap

Elbow

Union

Galvanized cross

Coupling

45° reducer elbow

Coupling

45° elbow

Brass drop-ear elbow, threaded

Reducer coupling

Tee

Street elbow

Tee

PE compression coupling

Selecting

To connect a faucet or toilet to a stop valve, choose among several types of supply tubes. **Plastic** tubes are inexpensive, but their thickness may restrict water flow. A solid **copper** or **chrome** tube, hollow or PEX-lined, must be cut to fit. A **braided stainless steel** or **braided plastic** supply tube is flexible and forgiving with respect to length. When buying a supply tube, be sure that one end will fit the stop valve, which has a ⅜- or ½-inch opening. The other end is sized to fit a faucet or a toilet. Buy a longer tube than you think is needed and cut or bend to fit.

Plastic

Copper

Lined chrome

Braided stainless steel

Braided plastic

Choosing plastic or copper/chrome traps

A trap uses thinner-gauge pipe, often called tubular pipe. The parts join together with slipnuts and washers so the trap can be easily taken apart for cleaning. A bathroom sink uses a 1¼-inch trap; a kitchen sink uses a 1½-inch trap.

A plastic trap will last nearly forever but is sometimes considered unsightly. When buying a chrome-plated copper trap, spend a bit more for one made of 17-gauge metal; thinner tubing may corrode within a couple of years.

DWV fittings

A plumbing inspector will pay close attention to DWV fittings, so be sure to list them in detail in your plan. Drain fittings make gradual turns to reduce the chance of clogs; vent fittings can make sharper turns.

A **90-degree drain elbow** is called a sweep or a quarter bend. **Quarter bends** are available in short, medium, or long radii; when in doubt, use the **long radius** if you have the room.

When working in a tight place, you can choose among a number of elbows, including a 60-degree, a 45-degree (or eighth bend), and a 22½-degree (or sixteenth bend).

When running a line for a toilet, be sure to use a special **closet bend**. It accepts a toilet flange that is installed after the finished floor surface is completed.

When coming out of the wall for a sink drain, use a **trap adapter;** the trap can be screwed directly onto it.

Tees and **Ys** of all sizes are available. The two openings opposite each other in a straight line are called the run openings; the other opening is the branch opening. When describing a tee, the run size is given first, then the branch size. For instance, a "4 by 3" tee or Y has two 4-inch run openings and one 3-inch branch opening. Always buy **waste tee** (sometimes called a "sanitary

tee"), which has a curved rather than an abrupt bend.

Crosses and **double-Ys** have two branch openings. A **reducer** or a **reducer bushing** connects different size pipes.

Codes require drain lines to have **cleanouts** at regular intervals. Install a Y with a cleanout plug or attach a cleanout plug to the end of a pipe.

To make a transition from galvanized steel to plastic drainpipe, use a plastic **male-to-threaded PVC coupling**. To join plastic to cast iron, use a special adapter fitting with a neoprene sleeve.

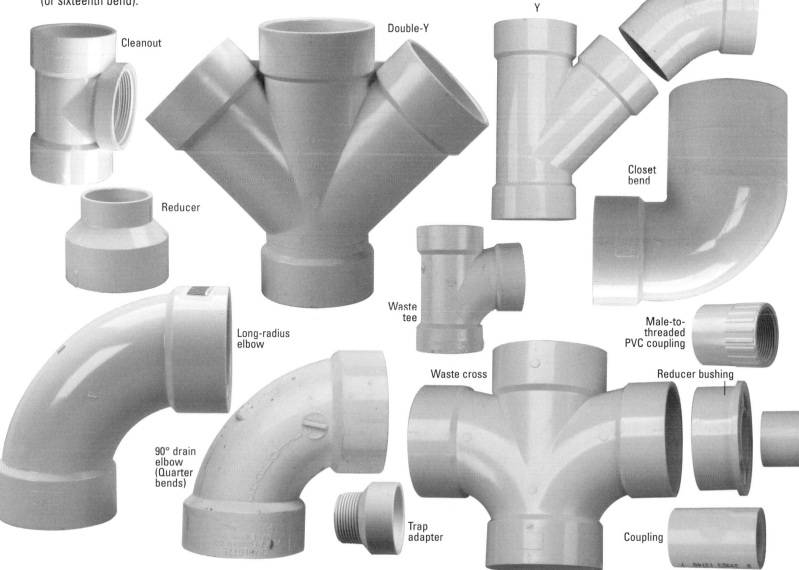

Cleanout

Double-Y

Y

45° bend

Reducer

Closet bend

Long-radius elbow

Waste tee

Male-to-threaded PVC coupling

90° drain elbow (Quarter bends)

Waste cross

Reducer bushing

Trap adapter

Coupling

MAPPING A HOME PLUMBING SYSTEM

Before attempting a major plumbing project, know your home's system. It may first appear to be a tangled web of hidden pipes, but you can soon learn where all the pipes go and what they do. Start by consulting the illustration on *page 9*, which has an overview of how plumbing systems work.

If you are fortunate enough to have a set of architectural drawings of your house that includes the plumbing, the job may be already done. However, plumbers often deviate from plans, so take some time to compare the plans to the actual pipes. If you have architectural drawings that do not show plumbing, make several copies and sketch in the existing plumbing. If you have no drawings, sketch your own. Later turn rough sketches into orderly drawings; *pages 26–27* show how.

Tips for finding pipes

If you still can't find all the pipes after following the steps at right, try these methods:

■ If an interior wall is thicker than the other walls (the usual thickness is 4 to 4½ inches), chances are good that it is a "wet wall" through which the main stack runs.

■ To find pipes in walls, turn on water and hold a stethoscope or a drinking glass against the wall surface. Supply pipes will hiss, and drainpipes will gurgle.

■ Turn off any intermediate shutoff valves and test to see which rooms they control.

■ If it is safe, climb onto your roof and run a hand-crank auger down through a vent pipe. Have a helper listen as you wiggle the auger. In this way you can map both the main and secondary vents.

■ If you have hot-water heat, map heating pipes separately. In older homes radiator pipes are usually larger than supply pipes, though they may resemble drainpipes. In a newer home, copper heat pipes (which carry water to convectors or to radiant-heat lines) may be ½- or ¾-inch copper and look just like supply pipes.

DWV map

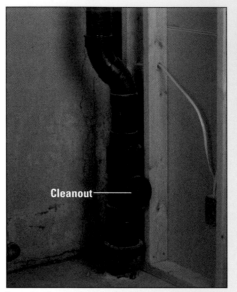

Locate the main stack, which is the largest-diameter pipe in a home. It should have a cleanout (near the floor in older homes, about 42 inches up in newer), which you can use to clean out the main drain line. The stack usually runs straight up to the roof but it may have an offset.

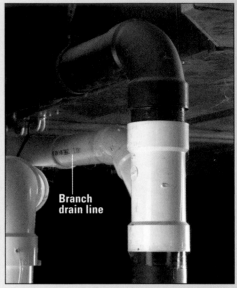

A secondary stack is a feature of most homes and often serves the kitchen. It also extends up through the roof, and it should have a cleanout. From a basement or crawlspace, you may be able to look up and see branch drain lines entering the stack.

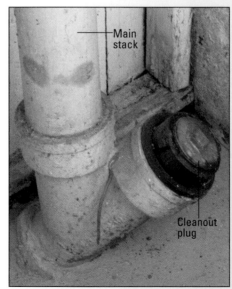

The main stack in an older home is a thick cast-iron pipe. It almost certainly travels straight up to the roof. It may have a cleanout plug like the one shown above, or there may be a cleanout hub on the floor.

A secondary stack in an older home is cast iron. Unlike the main stack, it may go around obstacles. Belowground, it may join directly with the main drain, or it may run to a common catch basin (see *page 11*).

To follow the course of the supply lines, start where the main line enters the house, and find the main shutoff *(page 6)*. Near the water heater, note where the single pipe branches off into hot and cold and how the hot/cold pairs branch off supplying different areas of the house.

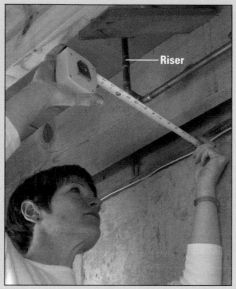

To trace the supply pipes further, determine where they enter the floor above. A supply pipe may run vertically with the wall (called a riser). However, its not unusual for the supply pipe to turn and run horizontal. Keep in mind that supply pipes must end up near drainpipes.

You'll likely find an access panel in the wall directly behind a shower (above) or bathtub's faucet. Remove the panel to expose the plumbing—it will provide valuable clues about how supply lines are routed.

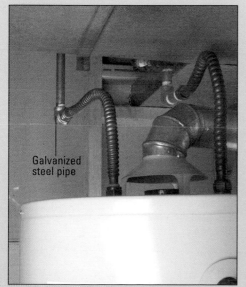

Older supply pipes are made of galvanized steel. If you see extensive rust at the joints, plan to replace the pipes. If water pressure is low in all or part of the house, mineral buildup may be the problem.

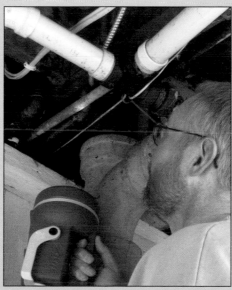

Take note of pipe sizes. Risers should be ¾ inch, but in many old homes they are only ½-inch, which can lead to low water pressure, especially if the pipes are galvanized steel.

You may find an access panel in a place other than behind a tub. Chances are such a panel was installed when a plumber had to make a repair.

PLUMBING CODES

Plumbing is the most complicated aspect of most bathroom and kitchen remodeling projects. It is essential that all the plumbing conform to code. Do-it-yourself plumbing that is done without benefit of inspections often turns out to be not only faulty, but dangerous and unhealthy.

The National Uniform Plumbing Code applies generally to the entire country, but local codes—which may be more stringent—most concern you. At the beginning of the planning process, visit or call your building department and obtain any printed information about local plumbing codes. Have the plans approved before starting work and perform all work to the satisfaction of the inspector (see opposite). Draw a detailed plan *(pages 26–27)* that includes a list of all materials.

Common codes

The first priority is venting. Can you revent, or do you need to send a new vent pipe up through the roof? Drainpipes that are not properly vented will run sluggishly and may release noxious fumes into the house. See *pages 10–11* for solutions to most venting problems. Here are some other important code considerations:

■ Fixtures must not be placed too close together. This is critical in a bathroom where space may be at a premium. See *pages 80–81* for regulations.

■ Determine the correct pipe sizes for drains, vents, and supply lines (see *page 25).*

■ Most inspectors will accept rigid copper pipe for supplies and PVC for drains.

■ To ensure adequate water pressure, you may need to replace an existing globe shutoff valve with a "full bore" ball or gate valve *(page 24),* which does not impede the flow of water. If pressure is very low, you may need a booster pump. Where pressure is too high, you may need a pressure-reducing valve.

■ The installation of plumbing must not weaken the structure of a house. The inspector may require that you reinforce joists that have been cut to accommodate pipes. Other requirements include the use of fire caulking around pipes and placement of protective plates over pipes.

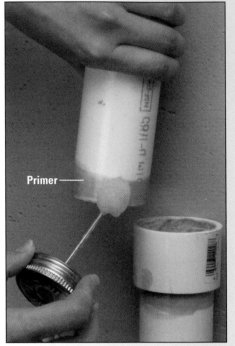

Use purple primer when joining PVC pipes so the inspector can quickly tell that the pipes have been primed. Pipes that are glued without primer will eventually leak.

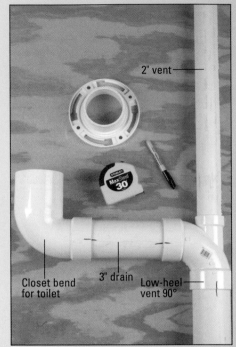

Purchase the right fittings by listing them in detail on your plan. Be sure to use special drain fittings (like the closet bend shown) so wastewater can flow smoothly. Inspectors will have very specific fitting requirements for different fixtures.

CORRECT SLOPE FOR DRAINPIPE

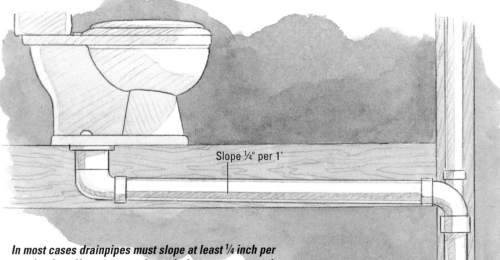

Slope ¼" per 1'

In most cases drainpipes must slope at least ¼ inch per running foot. If you are running a drain across a room that does not have a basement or crawlspace, this may call for careful calculations. Codes may require that vent pipes slope at ⅛ inch per foot, or they may permit you to install them level.

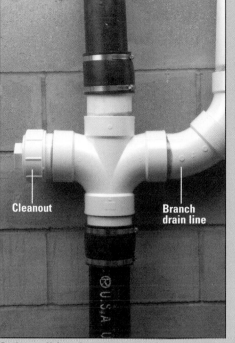

Cutting a notch in a joist greatly weakens it. So whenever possible, bore holes through joists instead. This calls for careful work; holes for drainpipe must be at slightly different levels so the pipe will slope. Whether notched or bored, long spans may need doubled joists (shown).

Codes call for cleanouts at various points so drains can be easily augered in case of a clog. To be safe, install a cleanout whenever you tap into a drain line unless there is already one nearby.

Once the drain lines are assembled, an inspector will probably test to make sure they do not leak. Some inspectors will simply pour water through the pipes. Other inspectors require that the line be plugged with an inflatable drain plug (shown above) and the system filled with water.

STANLEY PRO TIP: **Working with the building department**

Though it may seem a bother, working with your municipal building department ensures safe and reliable plumbing. When you sell your house, prospective buyers may be put off if they discover that work was done without inspection and may therefore be out of code. Many departments prefer to work with professionals and are skeptical of homeowners' ability to tackle advanced plumbing tasks. Here are some tips for getting off to the best possible start:

■ Find out if your building department requires a licensed plumber to run new plumbing lines. Some departments require a homeowner to pass a written or oral test before doing certain types of work.

■ The inspector's job is not to help plan but to inspect. An inspector may be willing to offer advice but don't ask, "What should I do?" Instead propose a plan and present it for feedback.

■ Draw up professional-quality plans, along with a complete list of materials *(pages 26–27)*. Make an appointment with the inspector to go over your plans. Listen carefully and take notes. Be polite and respectful but don't be afraid to ask questions if you do not understand.

■ Schedule inspections and be prepared for them. There will probably be two: one for the rough plumbing and one for the installation of fixtures. Don't make an appointment until the work is done—inspectors dislike coming back for a reinspection.

Above all, do not cover up any rough plumbing until the inspector has signed off on it. Doing so runs the risk of having to tear out brand-new walls to revise the plumbing.

WHAT IF...
You have a septic system?

If you live in a rural area, wastewater may drain into a septic system in the yard rather than flowing into a municipal sewage system. A typical septic system has three parts. Water flows first into a watertight septic tank, which retains the larger solids. Liquid with suspended smaller particles travels to a distribution box, which in turn sends the waste out to a series of perforated pipes. Waste liquid percolates through the pipes and into the ground.

If the system backs up, the tank may need to be pumped by a special service. Be sure you know where the tank is located; its lid may be buried.

If grass becomes very dark near the tank, the tank has probably cracked and needs to be replaced.

PLUMBING CODES (continued)

Valves, fixture controls, cleanouts, and compression pipe fittings must not be covered by a wall or floor surface. If you may need to work on the plumbing in the future, install an access panel. The most common location is behind a tub or shower *(page 21)*.

When changing pipe materials, use the correct transition fitting. Without a dielectric union (shown), the joint between galvanized and copper pipe would quickly corrode. Use the approved fitting when changing from plastic to copper, cast iron to plastic, and ABS to PVC.

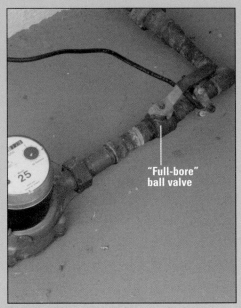

"Full-bore" ball valve

Old plumbing can usually remain; however, new plumbing needs to meet code. If old galvanized pipes and gate valves cause low water pressure, you may need to change them in order to supply the new pipes with enough pressure. As shown above, a newer ball valve has replaced a gate valve.

Hammer arrester

Codes may require a water hammer arrester near appliances such as a washing machine (shown), and perhaps at every faucet. Supply pipes may need to be cushioned wherever they run through or up against a framing member.

In addition to the main shutoff valve for a house, codes may require shutoff valves that control a portion of the house. A hose bib should have an interior shutoff valve. All faucets and toilets must have individual stop valves (see *page 6*). This corroded old valve will need replacement or repacking.

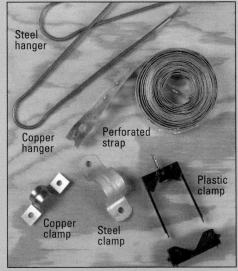

Steel hanger

Copper hanger

Perforated strap

Plastic clamp

Copper clamp

Steel clamp

Use approved clamps or straps to secure pipes. According to most codes, copper supply pipe must be supported every 6 feet; galvanized or black steel pipe every 12 feet; PVC or ABS drainpipe every 4 feet; cast-iron pipe every 5 feet. To be safe, install more supports than are required.

Water distribution pipes

Distribution pipes carry water from the main supply line to the rooms in the house, where they connect to branch lines.

Branch pipes

These pipes run from the distribution pipes to the fixtures. As a general rule, you can run ½-inch pipe to most fixtures; run ¾-inch pipe to a hose bib or a water heater.

Different fixtures place a different demand on supply pipes. Each fixture has a demand rating based on fixture units (see chart, right).

Supply tubes

These are the flexible lines that run from the stop valve to a faucet, fixture, or appliance. As a general rule, run ½-inch supply lines to all fixtures except toilets and bathroom sinks, which use ⅜-inch tubes.

DETERMINING SUPPLY FIXTURE UNITS

Add up the total number of fixture units in your house using this chart, then estimate how far the pipes travel inside your house.

Fixture	Units
Toilet	3
Bathroom sink	1
Tub/shower	2
Dishwasher	2
Kitchen sink	2
Washing machine	2
Hose bib	3

DETERMINING SUPPLY SIZE

Once you've totaled your home's fixture units, use this chart to check the minimum required size for the distribution pipes. Note that this chart is for estimating only. Local codes may vary, depending in part on the water pressure supplied by the utility.

Size of pipe from street	Size of distribution pipe	Length of pipe run/number of units			
		40'	60'	80'	100'
1"	1"	36	31	27	25
1"	¾"	33	28	25	23
¾"	1"	29	25	23	21
¾"	¾"	18	16	14	12
¾"	½"	6	5	4	4

Sizing drainpipes

Use the chart at right to count the number of fixture units that will be connected to a drain line, then see the chart at far right for the minimum drainpipe size. NOTE: If a toilet connects to a drainpipe, the pipe must be at least 3 inches. Check local codes.

Fixture trap size

A bathroom sink uses a 1¼-inch trap. Showers and floor drains use 2-inch traps. All other sinks and appliances use 1½-inch traps.

DETERMINING DRAIN FIXTURE UNITS

Fixture	Units
Shower/Tub	2
Bathroom sink	1
Toilet	3
Kitchen sink	2
Kitchen sink with disposer	3
Washing machine	2
Laundry sink	2
Floor Drain	2

DETERMINING DRAINPIPE SIZE

Pipe size	Maximum units, horizontal drainpipe	Maximum units, vertical drain stack
1¼"	1	2
1½"	3	4
2"	6	10
3"	20	30
4"	160	240

MAKING DRAWINGS

You may think that a rough sketch of a plumbing project is all you need. After all, you can figure out the details as you work, right? Even professional plumbers have to make on-the-fly changes after they start doing the work. The framing they find may differ from what they expected, or they may discover that their plan was faulty. Still the pros usually map a job in painstaking detail to avoid as many surprises as possible.

It's fairly easy to produce plan views and riser drawings that use official plumbing symbols. The effort expended making detailed drawings will save in time and expense later. The drawing process helps you think through the project in detail. That may enable you to spot a mistake you might otherwise overlook. It will almost certainly

minimize extra trips to the plumbing supply store. Also a clear, professional-quality plan will make your initial meeting with the building department more pleasant.

Getting started

A plan for a new plumbing service starts with a map of the existing plumbing; (see *pages 20–21).* Use color codes when drawing a plan to indicate the function of each pipe.

If you have architectural drawings, make several photocopies of them. If you have no architectural drawings, make several copies of an accurate scale drawing of the room.

The necessary tools are simple: a gridded straightedge like the one shown opposite will help you draw parallel lines. You'll also

need colored pencils, an eraser, and a 30-60-90-degree triangle.

Use grid paper so it's easy to establish a scale, like ½ inch to 6 or 12 inches. Such a scale makes it easy to note any problems with the layout and is a useful guide for estimating materials.

Final drawings

To make a plan drawing, first draw all fixtures to precise size and make sure they are not too close together (see *page 80).* Then put in the drain lines with fixtures; then the supplies. Make riser drawings as well.

Use the drawing to make a list of materials. Indicate the exact type of every fitting so the inspector can approve them. Indicate pipe sizes, including valves to match the pipe dimension.

Solid lines indicate drainpipes, and broken lines indicate hot and cold water lines. Because this is an overhead view, notes must indicate any vertical runs. Different colored pencil lines make clear the function of each pipe. All pipe sizes are shown with a curled leader line to avoid confusion. Expect to make several versions of your plan—better to make your mistakes on paper than on the job site.

Photocopy the floor plan
For complex projects, draw your floor plan, then make several photocopies. This allows you to sketch out several trial plans.

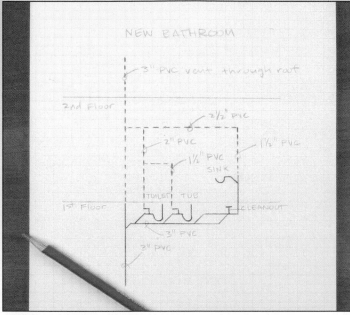

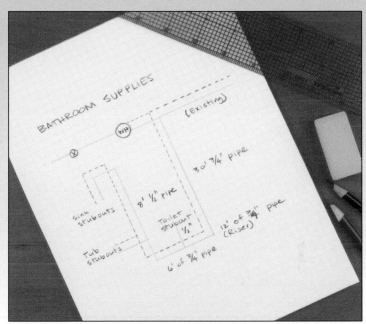

A DWV elevation describes the upward path of the stack, vents and revents, the length of drainpipe runs, and traps. Its primary purpose is to show how the fixtures will be vented. It doesn't have to be drawn over an architectural drawing.

A supply drawing indicates the estimated length of supply pipes. The main purpose is to determine the minimum size of the pipes (see the chart on *page 25*).

Plumbing symbols

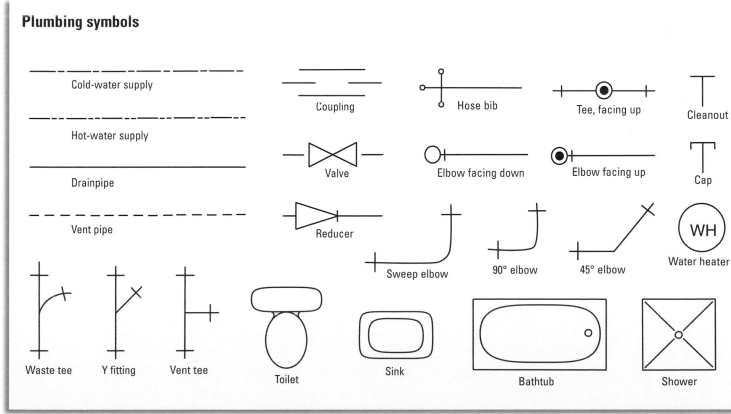

PLUMBING SKILLS

Cutting and joining the various types of pipe—copper, plastic, and steel—calls for special techniques. These methods can be learned in an hour or two. This chapter teaches you how to work with the materials you choose.

Practice, practice
Though you may never learn to install plumbing as quickly as a professional plumber, with practice you can make joints that are every bit as strong and durable as those made by the pros. But these techniques take practice, so buy extra pipe and fittings and practice cutting until you can make straight cuts. Experiment to find out how far a pipe pokes into a fitting so you can measure accurately. Clamp a pipe to a vise on a workbench and join it to a fitting. Keep practicing until you are confident that your joints are tight and secure.

Preparing the work site
Working in tight spots is usually what makes plumbing difficult. Evaluate the working conditions and take time to make things as comfortable as possible. Remove all obstructions. Place a bucket under any pipe that might leak as it is disassembled. In confined spaces, have plenty of large towels on hand to soak up spilled water and to cushion your back, head, and knees. Protect floors with a thick drop cloth.

You may need to pull an existing pipe away from a wall or framing member in order to cut and join a new line to it.

Remove a clamp or strap or two and pull gently. Copper pipe can kink if you pull it too hard. Unscrewing a steel pipe fitting can stress corroded threads enough to cause a leak.

Before working on any project, practice the golden rule of plumbing: **Shut off the water** and test to make sure the water is off. When working on DWV pipes, shut off the water, flush all the toilets, and tell household members not to use the drainage system.

Make the job site safe. When sweating copper pipe, protect all flammable surfaces and have a fire extinguisher ready. When working on a drain line, keep the room ventilated in case noxious fumes escape. **Shut off a gas line before working on it.**

Installing new plumbing requires skills that can be learned in just an hour or two.

CHAPTER PREVIEW

Working with copper pipe
page 30

Installing plastic drainpipe
page 32

CPVC and flexible plastic
page 34

Installing steel pipe
page 36

PVC and copper pipe are relatively inexpensive so buy more than you think you'll need to allow for mistakes.

Advanced plumbing projects call for special preparations. Clear away furniture and lay down a thick, absorbent drop cloth. A drop cloth will protect the floor from dropped tools and fittings. In addition it will soak up any residual water and catch any spilled primer, putty, and debris.

Working with cast-iron pipe
page 38

Running through walls and floors
page 40

Connecting new to old
page 42

WORKING WITH COPPER PIPE

A properly soldered (or "sweated") joint on copper pipe is as strong as the pipe itself. However, a poorly soldered joint will leak the next day, or in a year or two.

The trick is to work systematically because each step depends on the previous one: The pipe must be cut straight and all burrs removed. The inside of the fitting and the outside of the pipe must be brushed or sanded to a shine. Flux must be applied for the solder to adhere. The solder must be fully drawn into the joint. Even wiping is essential: a droplet of solder can weaken a joint.

Keep it round

Pipe ends and fittings must be perfectly round. If either is dented or even slightly flattened, it is all but impossible to restore the original roundness. Cut the pipe again or buy a new fitting.

Cutting with a tubing cutter ensures roundness. If space is tight and you must cut with a hacksaw, do it slowly and gently. If you must bend a pipe to move it away from a wall, work carefully.

Felt-tipped marker

1 Hold a pipe in place to measure for a cut or use a tape measure. Take into account the distance the pipe will travel into the fitting. Mark with a felt-tipped marker or a pencil.

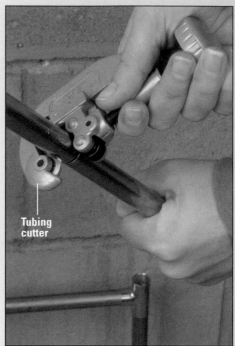

Tubing cutter

2 Use a large tubing cutter or a small one if space is tight *(page 43)*. Align the cutting wheel with the cut mark. Twist the knob until the wheel starts to bite into the pipe. Rotate the cutter once, tighten a half turn or so, and repeat until the pipe is cut. Assemble all the parts of a joint in a dry run.

PRESTART CHECKLIST

☐ **TIME**
About 15 minutes to cut a pipe and join a fitting

☐ **TOOLS**
Tubing cutter or hacksaw, multiuse wire brush, propane torch (preferably with a trigger igniter), flux brush, groove-joint pliers, flame guard

☐ **SKILLS**
Cutting pipe, soldering

☐ **PREP**
Protect any flammable surfaces with a fiber shield or a cookie sheet.

☐ **MATERIALS**
Copper pipe and fittings, flux, solder (95 percent tin for drinking water supply), damp rag

Sweating a brass valve

Meltable parts

If a valve has any plastic parts—as is the case with most stop valves—disassemble the valve and remove all the meltable parts. Heat the brass valve body as you would a fitting. It may take a bit longer to heat than a fitting. After sweating, wait for the valve to cool before replacing the plastic parts.

STANLEY PRO TIP

Protect walls and framing from the torch flame

While caught up in the sweating process you may not notice that the flame is charring a joist or wall surface. Protect flammable surfaces with a fiber flame guard *(page 14)* or use an old cookie sheet or two. **Keep a home fire extinguisher handy.**

If you can't pull a pipe more than a half inch away from a wall or framing member, don't worry about heating all around the fitting. As long as you heat two opposite sides, the solder will draw evenly around the joint.

Avoid MAPP gas an alternative to propane fuel. It produces an extremely hot flame not recommended for most residential work.

After the job is complete, **check the area an hour later to be sure no flammable surfaces are smoldering.**

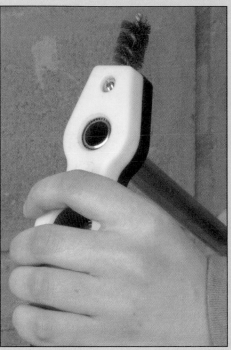

3 Using a wire brush made for the size of the fitting, ream out every inside opening until it is shiny. Oil from your hand may weaken the joint. If you accidentally touch a brushed opening, ream it again.

4 Brush or sand the outside of the pipe to be joined until it shines by inserting the pipe end in the multiuse brush and spinning the brush a few times. Re-brush or re-sand if you touch the shiny area.

5 Using the flux brush (it often comes with the can of flux), apply flux to all the inside openings of the fitting and to the outside of the pipe. Take care to keep the flux brush away from any debris; clean it if any particles stick to it.

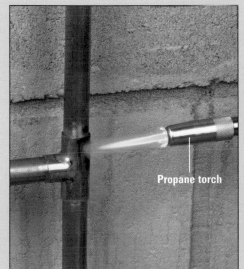

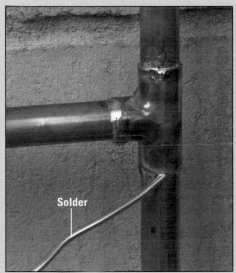

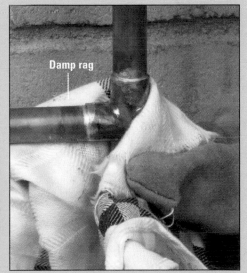

6 Ignite a propane torch and point the flame at the fitting near the joint—not at the pipe and not at the joint. The tip of the blue portion of the flame should just touch the fitting. Move the flame back and forth so you heat two opposite sides of the fitting.

7 When the fitting starts to smoke, remove the flame and touch the tip of the solder to the joint. If it does not melt, heat again. Once the fitting is hot enough, the solder will be drawn into the joint. Move the solder around so the entire joint is soldered.

8 Immediately repeat the process for any other joints in the fitting. This will go quickly because the fitting is already hot. Once all the joints are soldered, quickly wipe all the joints with a damp rag. Avoid bumping the fitting for 10 to 15 minutes.

INSTALLING PLASTIC DRAINPIPE

Plastic PVC pipe and fittings are inexpensive and easy to install. However, do not take this work lightly. Once glued together, a joint is rock-hard and cannot be adjusted. If you make a mistake, you'll have to cut out the section and start all over again.

Making a dry run
To prevent a mistake, cut and assemble the pipes in a dry run: Cut and temporarily join five or six pipes and fittings together and make sure that the last pipe in the run is facing the right direction. Use a felt-tipped pen to make alignment marks on all the joints where the fitting must face correctly. Disassemble, keeping careful track of the order of installation. Apply primer to each pipe end and each fitting. Apply cement and join each pipe in order.

PRESTART CHECKLIST

☐ **TIME**
About an hour to cut and assemble five or six pipes and fittings

☐ **TOOLS**
PVC saw or backsaw and miter box or power miter saw, deburring tool, felt-tipped marker

☐ **SKILLS**
Sawing, measuring, working methodically

☐ **PREP**
Make a drawing of the drain/vent assembly and clear a path for the pipes.

☐ **MATERIALS**
Primer and cement for your type and size of pipe (see *opposite*)

Plastic-pipe saw   Miter box

Deburring tool

1 When measuring, allow for the distance the pipe will travel inside the fitting. Use a felt-tipped marker to mark the pipe. You can use a hacksaw or backsaw to cut PVC, but a plastic pipe saw is easier to use. A power miter saw with a fine-cutting blade is easiest of all. Cut it square.

2 Remove all the burrs from the cut pipe end. You can do this by scraping with a knife, but a deburring tool does a better job and is easier to use. Assemble cut pipes and fittings in a dry run (see *below*).

DRY RUN FOR DRAINPIPE

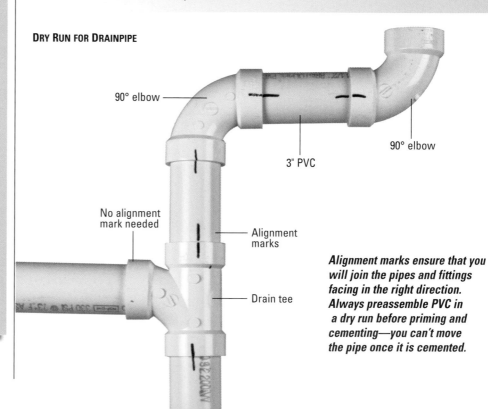

90° elbow

90° elbow

3" PVC

No alignment mark needed

Alignment marks

Drain tee

Alignment marks ensure that you will join the pipes and fittings facing in the right direction. Always preassemble PVC in a dry run before priming and cementing—you can't move the pipe once it is cemented.

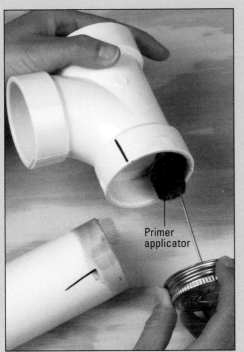

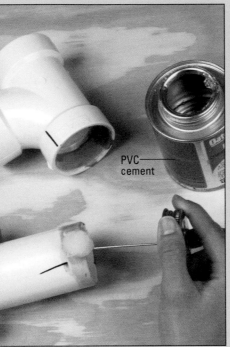

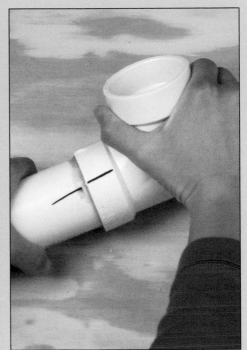

3 Apply primer to the inside of the fitting openings and to the pipe ends. The applicator should be wet enough to produce a fairly dark line, but not so wet that the primer drips. Place the pieces where they will not get dirty. If debris sticks to the primer, it will be difficult to join the pipes.

4 Apply cement to the inside of one fitting opening and the end of one pipe. Work quickly—cement starts to set up in a few seconds.

5 Push the pipe into the fitting, and twist so the alignment marks line up. Hold for a few seconds, then wipe with a damp cloth. In a minute, the joint will be strong enough so you can assemble the next piece. After 15 minutes, you can run unpressurized wastewater through the pipes.

WHAT IF...
You are connecting ABS pipe?

Most codes require PVC for drain lines; but if you already have black ABS pipe in your home, local codes may allow you to add to your system using the same material instead of making a transition to PVC.

Cut and assemble the black ABS pipe in much the same way as you would PVC pipe. Use a plastic-cutting saw or backsaw with a miter box, remove the burrs, and put pipe and fittings together in a dry run. Use a sharpened, light-colored crayon to make alignment marks.

Instead of primer, apply ABS cleaner to pipe ends and fitting openings. Use special ABS cement to glue the pieces together. Push the pieces together and twist.

To connect PVC pipe to existing ABS pipe, use a no-hub fitting (page 42).

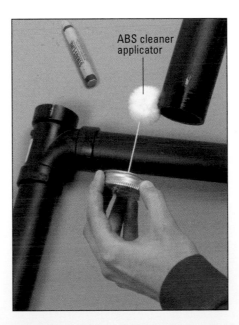

Use the right products

Check the label on a can of primer or cement to make sure it's made for your type of pipe. Local inspectors may or may not approve of "all-purpose" cement. The larger the pipe's diameter, the bigger the applicator should be so you won't have to dip it twice. As a general rule, an applicator should be about half the diameter of the pipe to be joined.

WORKING WITH CPVC AND FLEXIBLE PLASTIC

Check local codes before installing any type of plastic supply pipe; many building departments do not permit it for interior installations.

However, CPVC and other types of extra-strong plastic pipe are often used for irrigation systems and other outdoor installations. Because plastic pipe can be cracked when bumped (say, by a lawn mower), some codes allow it only for underground installations and require metal pipe aboveground.

Often rigid plastic supply pipe is used with flexible tubing such as PEX, both for outdoor and interior installations. In a typical irrigation system, rigid pipe is used for long runs, and flexible tubing is used for shorter runs leading to sprinkler heads or bubblers.

PRESTART CHECKLIST

☐ **TIME**
About an hour to cut and join five or six pieces of pipe and fittings

☐ **TOOLS**
Scissors-type plastic pipe cutter or plastic-pipe saw and miter box, deburrer, plastic tubing cutter, adjustable wrench

☐ **SKILLS**
Cutting, measuring, cementing

☐ **PREP**
Cut holes behind walls or under floors to clear a path for the supply pipes.

☐ **MATERIALS**
Plastic supply pipe approved by local codes, appropriate primer and cement, damp rag, flexible pipe, compression fittings

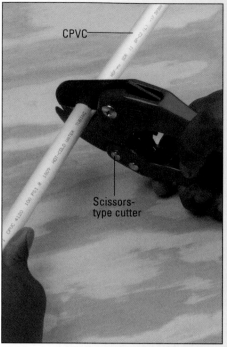

CPVC

Scissors-type cutter

Deburring tool

1 Measure for the desired length and mark the pipe with a felt-tipped marker. Cut small-diameter plastic pipe with a scissors-type cutter (shown) or use a saw and miter box.

2 Scissor cutters cut cleanly; but if you use a saw or there are any burrs, use a deburring tool to smooth the inside and outside of the cut end. Dry-fit the pipes and make alignment marks.

PLASTIC PIPE SYSTEM

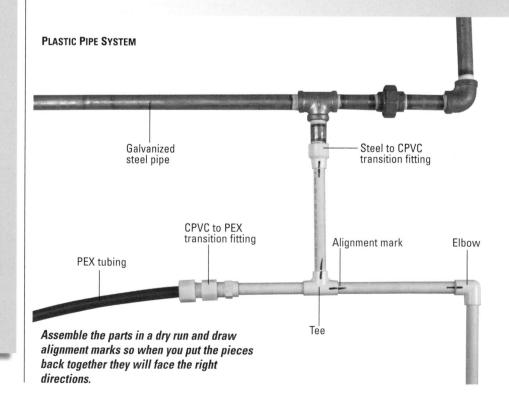

Galvanized steel pipe

Steel to CPVC transition fitting

CPVC to PEX transition fitting

Alignment mark

Elbow

PEX tubing

Tee

Assemble the parts in a dry run and draw alignment marks so when you put the pieces back together they will face the right directions.

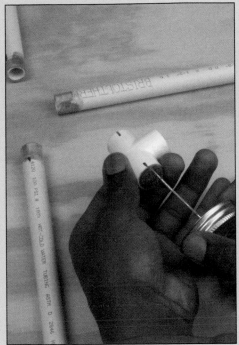

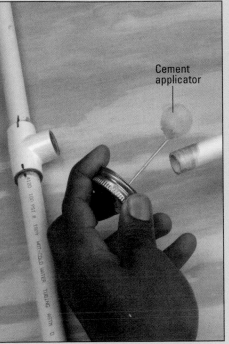

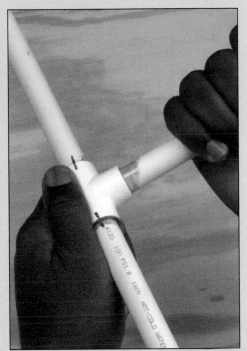

3 Using a small can with a small applicator brush, apply purple primer to the inside of the fitting and to the pipe end. Place the pieces on a surface where they will not get dirty.

4 One pipe and fitting at a time, apply cement to the inside of the fitting and to the pipe end.

5 Quickly insert the pipe into the joint and twist. Where there are alignment marks, make sure they meet. Hold for a few seconds and then wipe the joint with a damp rag.

Joining PEX pipe

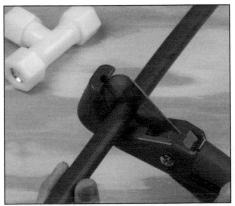

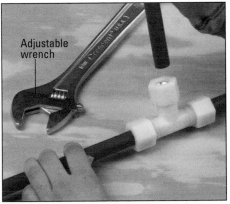

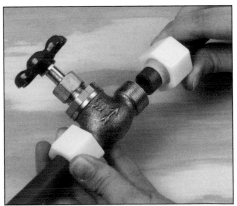

1 Flexible supply pipe—most commonly PEX—is approved in many areas for indoor and outdoor use. Check local codes; you may be allowed to run only the tubing through walls, while all fittings have to be accessible. Cut with a plastic-tubing cutter.

2 Purchase fittings made for your type of tubing. To connect, simply push the tubing into the fitting and tighten the nut with an adjustable wrench.

3 Use a special nut (that has its own ferrule) to connect to valves and fixtures. Slide the nut onto the tubing, push the tubing into the valve inlet, slide the nut to the valve, and tighten the nut with an adjustable wrench.

Installing Steel Pipe

New water supply lines are usually copper or plastic; but if your home has galvanized pipe and you need to replace a leaky section of pipe or add a short run, it makes sense to use the same material.

Almost all gas lines are black threaded pipe, which is installed the same way as galvanized pipe (see opposite).

Buying materials

Don't try to cut and thread steel pipe yourself. Measure carefully, keeping in mind that ½- and ¾-inch pipe goes about ½ inch into each fitting. Then have a home center or hardware store cut and thread pieces to these exact measurements.

A more flexible strategy is to estimate your pipe and fitting needs. Then you can buy long pipes as well as a variety of "nipples"—short lengths of threaded pipe ranging from 1 to 12 inches. Also buy extra couplings. When you come close to the end of a run, you can probably create the correct length by combining nipples and couplings.

Prestart Checklist

☐ **Time**
About an hour to cut into a line and install several fittings and pipes

☐ **Tools**
Two pipe wrenches (14-inch wrenches are a good choice), groove-joint pliers, hacksaw or reciprocating saw

☐ **Skills**
Careful measuring and planning, firm tightening using a pipe wrench

☐ **Prep**
Shut off water to the pipe you will break into. If you can find a nearby union fitting, you may be able to avoid cutting a pipe.

☐ **Materials**
Threaded pipe lengths and nipples, pipe-thread tape or pipe joint compound

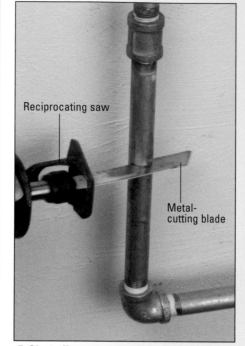

Reciprocating saw

Metal-cutting blade

1 **Shut off water to the line.** To tap into the middle of a line when there is no nearby union fitting, cut through a pipe with a reciprocating saw equipped with a metal-cutting blade or with a hacksaw. Unscrew the pipe on both sides of the cut.

Pipe-thread tape

2 Before threading a pipe into a fitting, wrap the threads with several windings of pipe-thread tape. With the pipe end facing you, wrap clockwise. Or, brush pipe joint compound onto the threads of both the pipe end and the inside of the fitting.

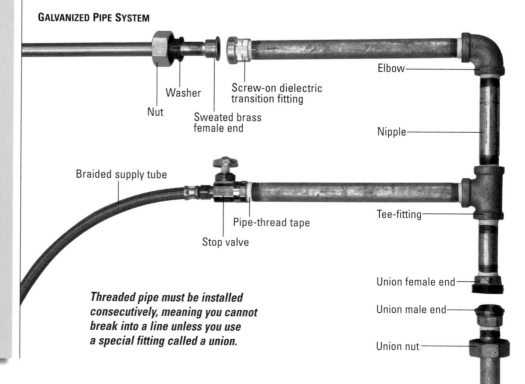

Galvanized Pipe System

Nut

Washer

Screw-on dielectric transition fitting

Sweated brass female end

Elbow

Nipple

Braided supply tube

Pipe-thread tape

Stop valve

Tee-fitting

Union female end

Union male end

Union nut

Threaded pipe must be installed consecutively, meaning you cannot break into a line unless you use a special fitting called a union.

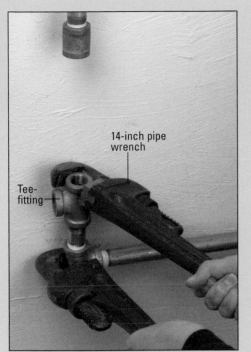

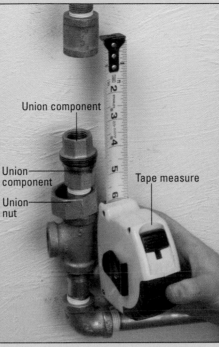

3 Twist on a pipe or fitting by hand. If it does not turn easily, the joint is not straight and the threads are crossed. Back up and try again. Then firmly tighten each pipe or fitting in turn, using a 14-inch pipe wrench. You may need a second wrench to hold the adjacent piece steady.

4 Once the tee-fitting for the new line is installed, add a nipple and slip on the nut for the union, checking that the threads are toward the joint. Apply tape and install half of the union. Set the second half of the union in place and measure for the final section of pipe.

5 Attach the second half of the union to the final piece and install. The union halves should line up so they can seat against each other. Slip the union nut up and hand-tighten. Then fully tighten the nut with a pipe wrench to complete the union.

Dielectric fitting for transition to copper

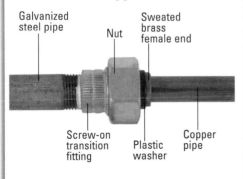

To install a dielectric union, screw the threaded part onto the steel pipe. Before sweating the brass fitting of the copper pipe, slip on the nut and sleeve then push them well away from the heat of the torch. Once the fitting is sweated and cools, join the two parts. Use only groove-joint pliers to tighten the nut.

STANLEY PRO TIP: **Safely joining black gas pipe**

1 Before working with black threaded gas pipe, **shut off the gas** and ventilate the room. Follow the steps shown above, but use black pipe and fittings instead of galvanized. Wrap threaded ends with special yellow pipe-thread tape, made for use with gas pipe.

2 After installation, turn the gas back on and test for leaks. Spray gas-joint testing fluid, or brush liquid soap (shown above) or soapy water on a joint. If you see bubbles, there is a leak. Tightening the nipple or valve will likely stop the leak. Retest.

WORKING WITH CAST-IRON DRAINPIPE

If a section of cast-iron pipe needs replacing, or if you want to tap into a cast-iron pipe with a new drain line, don't install more cast-iron pipe. Instead, make the transition to PVC drainpipe.

Several types of no-hub fittings are available; check local codes to see which are accepted. A no-hub fitting has a neoprene sleeve and clamps that are tightened around the cast-iron pipe and the plastic replacement piece to hold them in place and make a watertight joint. Such fittings are considered a permanent joint.

Cast-iron pipe is extremely heavy, so work carefully and use a helper. Never move or cut a piece until you are sure it is adequately supported with clamps and perhaps with framing as well. Add clamps above and below the new joint or leave frame permanently in place.

PRESTART CHECKLIST

☐ **TIME**
A full day to support, cut, and install a replacement piece with two banded couplings; an hour or two to install a saddle-tee fitting (opposite)

☐ **TOOLS**
Carpentry tools, cast-iron snap cutter or circular saw with metal-cutting blade, hex screwdriver or torque wrench, tools for installing plastic drainpipe (page 32)

☐ **SKILLS**
Good carpentry skills, measuring, attaching with bolts

☐ **PREP**
Examine how the existing pipe is clamped and determine how best to hold it firmly as you work.

☐ **MATERIALS**
Plastic pipe or fitting matching cast-iron pipe, banded couplings, riser clamps

1 **Secure the pipe above and below the point that will be cut** so that neither end can fall or move sideways while you work. To be safe, build a frame like the one shown here and attach the pipe to it with riser clamps.

2 Next to a snap cutter (below), the quickest way to cut cast iron is with a circular saw equipped with a metal-cutting blade. **Wear eye and ear protection.** If a circular saw will not reach all the way around, cut all or part with a reciprocating saw equipped with a metal-cutting blade.

STANLEY PRO TIP: **Make a quick, clean break with a snap cutter**

Another way to cut cast-iron pipe is with a snap cutter, which can be rented. After supporting the pipe above and below, wrap the cutter's chains around the pipe. Each chain link has a little wheel cutter. Follow manufacturer's instructions. Typically a handle sets the ratchet for loosening or tightening. Set it for tightening; pump the lever slowly until the chain is tight. Continue ratcheting until the cutting wheels crack through the pipe. Cut both sides and, wearing gloves, remove the scrap piece of pipe.

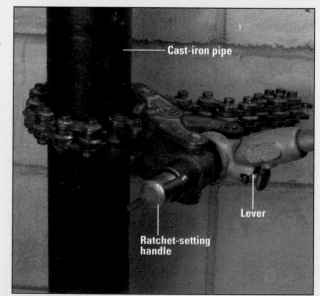

No-hub fitting

Y-fitting with short pieces of pipe installed

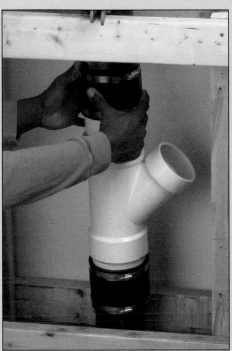

Hex screwdriver

3 To install a tee or Y, glue two short pieces of pipe to each end of the fitting *(pages 32–33)*, making sure the resulting component will fit snugly between the pipes. Slip the no-hub fitting onto each of the cast-iron pipe ends.

4 Position the fitting or replacement piece between the two cut cast iron ends and pull the neoprene sleeve over the plastic.

5 At each joint slide the neoprene sleeve of the no-hub fitting so it's centered on the joint. Tighten the band nuts using a hex screwdriver. Some codes may require the use of a torque wrench, which will stop tightening when you reach the proper band tightness.

Installing a saddle-tee drain fitting

Grinder with metal-cutting blade

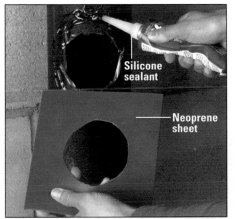

Silicone sealant

Neoprene sheet

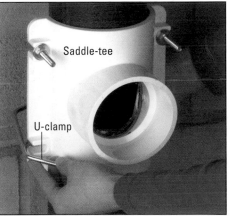

Saddle-tee

U-clamp

1 If it's approved by your local inspector, a saddle fitting is easier and quicker to install. Cut a roughly circular hole in the cast-iron pipe using a grinder equipped with a metal-cutting blade (shown). The hole should be slightly larger than the opening in the fitting.

2 Hold a neoprene sheet for the fitting against the hole and trace the outline of the hole. Cut a hole in the sheet that's slightly larger than the hole in the pipe. Squeeze silicone sealant around the hole.

3 Position the sheet over the hole and press the plastic fitting over it. Slip a U-clamp over the back of the pipe and slide its threaded ends through the plastic fitting. Screw on the two nuts finger-tight. Attach the other clamp the same way, then tighten all four nuts.

RUNNING PIPES THROUGH WALLS AND FLOORS

Once you've drawn a plan for new plumbing service and have had it approved, develop a strategy for running those pipes. If you are lucky enough to work in a new building or addition where all the framing is exposed, this is fairly easy. If you are remodeling, be prepared for a few surprises and slight changes in plan once you've removed some of the wall surface and flooring.

Removing wall and floor surfaces prior to plumbing takes about half a day of hard work. But replacing finished surfaces after plumbing (especially patching walls) usually takes several days. A large wall patch—even replacing an entire wall—takes little more time than a small patch, so open up plenty of space for working.

Once you've opened up the vent and drain lines, running the supplies—which usually run alongside DWV (Drain-Waste-Vent) lines—will be relatively easy.

PRESTART CHECKLIST

☐ **TIME**
For a modest bathroom, two or three days to cut into walls and flooring and run pipes through framing

☐ **TOOLS**
Demolition tools, drill with various bits and hole saws, reciprocating saw, level, tools for installing pipe

☐ **SKILLS**
Carpentry, knowledge of your home's structure, installing pipe

☐ **PREP**
Have your plan approved by the local building department.

☐ **MATERIALS**
Pipes, fittings, clamps, and assembly materials listed on your plan

Cutout for new stack

1 If you need to run a new stack (see *pages 10–11)*, assess your framing. An installation with a toilet must have a 3-inch drain, which can be installed only if the stud wall is made of 2×6s or larger. (Two-inch pipe can be run through a 2×4 wall.) Remove the wall surface up to the ceiling.

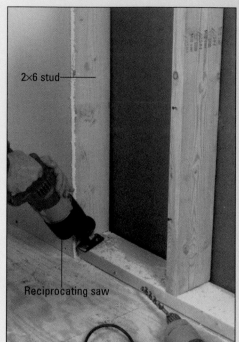

2×6 stud

Reciprocating saw

2 Cut a hole with some wiggle room for the new pipe. For a 3-inch pipe, use a drill and reciprocating saw to cut a hole about 4¼ inches by 10 inches through both the bottom plate of the room you are working in and the top plate of the room below. Cut away a 10-inch by 2-foot section of flooring.

Stabilizing and protecting pipes

Shim

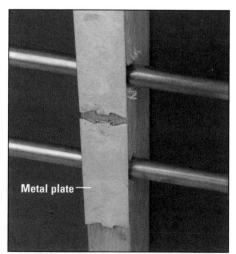

Metal plate

Whenever possible, run pipes through holes in the center of framing members. To keep pipes from rattling, line the holes with felt or use wood shims. Slip a shim under the pipe and tap in until it is firmly in place, but not tight, to allow for expansion.

If notches are needed, make them as small as possible; they weaken the framing member. Protect pipes from nails by attaching metal plates.

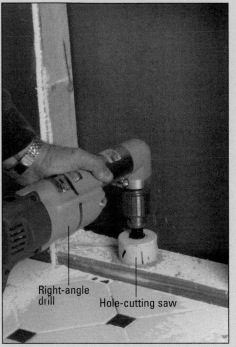

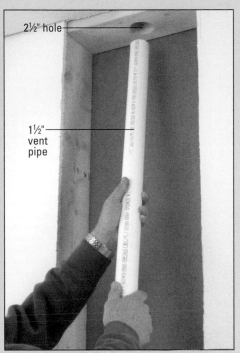

3 Assemble the approved fittings onto the top of the drainpipe. Take special care that they face the right direction. The drainpipe should be longer than needed—you can cut it to size from below later. Slip the pipe down through the hole.

4 You may need to cut a hole in the wall of the room above or below to guide the vent pipe up or the drainpipe down. In the attic, you may be able to run the vent over to tie into an existing vent. If not, drill a hole in the attic ceiling and have a roofer install a roof jack for the vent pipe.

5 Anchor the drainpipe with straps. Cut a smaller opening in the ceiling for the vent pipe. For a 1½-inch vent pipe, a 2½-inch hole is sufficient. Guide the vent pipe up through the hole and into the attic or room above and slip its lower end into the fitting at the floor.

Running pipe through a floor

Running drainpipe through joists calls for meticulous work. The holes must follow a straight line across the floor and must ascend or descend so the pipe will be sloped ¼ inch per foot. (If joists are 16 inches on center and pipes run across them at a right angle, holes should differ in height by about ⅜ inch.)

Running pipe through walls

Vent pipes may run level, though some codes may call for a slight slope toward the main drain. All drain lines must be sloped. For a precise slope, strike a level line on the studs and measure down ¼ inch per running foot. Codes may call for fireproof caulking in walls.

CONNECTING NEW TO OLD

Whether installing a new drain, vent, or supply line, the most common way to tie into an existing line is to cut the old line and install a tee-fitting. If you happen to find a pipe that is capped at its end, simply install an elbow or coupling there instead.

Shut off water to existing supply pipes and drain the lines. Flush all toilets and caution others not to use drains. After opening a drain line, make sure no one uses a sink or faucet that drains into it. Seal any open drain lines with a large rag to protect against fumes.

If joining pipes of different materials, make sure the transition fitting conforms to local code.

Typically it doesn't matter exactly where you join to an existing pipe, but the new service must be precisely located. So it's usually easier to start pipe runs at the new location and travel toward the existing pipes rather than vice versa.

PRESTART CHECKLIST

☐ **TIME**
Once pipes are run, usually less than two hours to connect new to old

☐ **TOOLS**
Cutting and fitting tools for any type of pipe you will be working with, carpentry tools, reciprocating saw, hex-head driver

☐ **SKILLS**
Cutting and joining the type of pipe used in the project

☐ **PREP**
Run new pipes from the new service location to the existing pipe. Install the last pipe a little longer than it needs to be so you can cut it to length when you make the connection to the old pipe.

☐ **MATERIALS**
Joining materials for the type of pipe you will work on, transition fittings

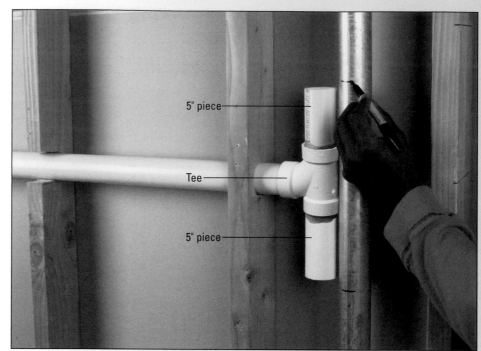

5" piece — Tee — 5" piece

1 To join a new plastic drainpipe to an old steel pipe, run new pipe into the room. Prime and glue two 5-inch pieces of pipe to a tee-fitting. Temporarily run pipe—longer than it needs to be—so it comes near the old pipe. (When running pipe across a stud wall, you may need to notch-cut some of the holes, using a reciprocating saw.) Dry-fit the tee assembly onto the new pipe and hold it next to the existing pipe. Mark the existing pipe for cutting. You may need to cut the opening larger than the tee assembly to accommodate the neoprene sleeves on the banded couplings.

WHAT IF...
You need to connect new PVC to old ABS?

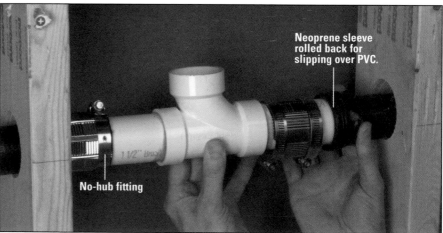

Neoprene sleeve rolled back for slipping over PVC.

No-hub fitting

Even though there are specialty primers and cements intended for joining PVC pipe to an old ABS line, local codes may not permit connecting in this manner. Instead use a no-hub fitting, which has a neoprene sleeve and metal clamps, to hold it firm. Some municipalities may require that the fitting be accessible for future repairs.

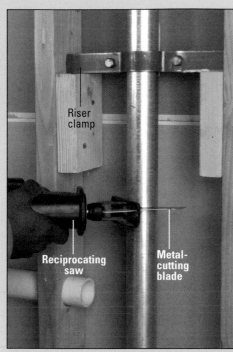

2 Support the pipe above and below with riser clamps so it cannot drop or sway as you work, and so the PVC fitting will not have to bear the weight of the drain. You will probably need to install a new stud or two as well as blocking for the upper clamp.

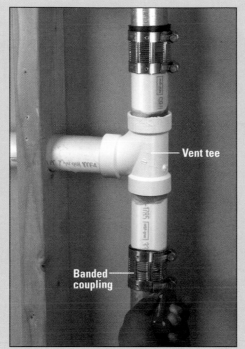

3 Slide a no-hub fitting onto each end of the old pipe, slide back the banded coupling, and fold up the neoprene sleeves. Position the tee assembly. Fold the neoprene sleeves over the assembly and slide the metal bands over the sleeves. Tighten the nuts with a hex-head driver.

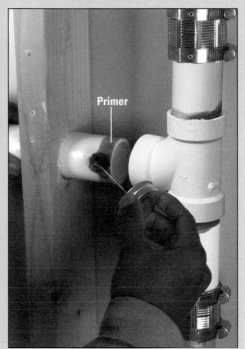

4 Cut the new pipe to exact length and test that it fits into the tee-fitting; you may need to loosen the nuts and rotate the fitting slightly. Prime and glue the pipe to the fitting *(page 33)*.

Tapping into supply lines

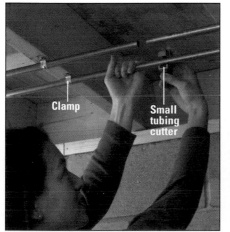

To tap into existing copper lines, shut off the water. With a tubing cutter, cut an opening in each pipe that is about an inch shorter than a tee-fitting. Dry-fit the tees. If the pipes are rigidly installed, remove a clamp or two so you can pull the pieces apart slightly.

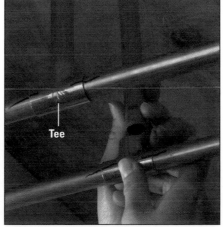

Dry-fit the pipes that will be inserted into the tees and draw alignment marks. Disassemble, wire-brush the fittings and pipe ends, brush on flux, and sweat the joints (see *pages 30–31*).

Joining copper to existing galvanized pipe

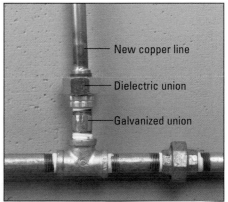

To tie a new copper line into an old galvanized line, follow the steps on *pages 36–37* for installing a new galvanized tee-fitting. Screw a galvanized nipple into the tee and connect the copper line to the nipple using a dielectric union *(page 37)*.

REPLACING TUBS AND SHOWERS

Bathtubs and showers sustain heavy use and are frequently scoured, so it's not surprising they eventually need to be replaced. This chapter shows how to remove an old tub and install a new one, as well as how to spruce up a tub or shower enclosure. If you need to install a new tub or shower with new plumbing, see the chapter "Installing a New Bathroom."

Some inspectors don't require an inspection for fixture replacements. As long as no new drain or supply pipes are to be installed, no permit will be required.

But check with your building department; this is a major job. It's to your benefit to have an inspector sign off on it. If you are running new lines for a shower *(pages 54–57)*, be sure to schedule inspections.

Plan the whole job
Replacing a tub or installing a shower is a remodeling project, involving not only plumbing but also carpentry, wall repair, and perhaps tiling. Count the cost and prepare for all aspects of the job. Allow yourself plenty of time. Just patching and painting a wall can take several days.

Leaks below a bathroom
If water drips from the ceiling below a bathroom, incompletely sealed walls and floors or cracked tiles are usually the cause—not necessarily the plumbing. Even a small gap in caulking or grout can provide a pathway for stray shower and bath water. By the time you notice a leak, there may be serious damage to walls, ceilings, and framing members. Every few months, inspect the grout and caulk. Encourage family members to dry off in the tub or to use an absorbent rug so that water does not puddle on the floor.

Replacing a tub or installing a shower is a major project that can take more than a week.

CHAPTER PREVIEW

Removing a tub
page 46

Replacing a tub
page 49

Installing a prefab tub surround
page 52

Building a shower enclosure
page 54

Cavity cut out for
tub installation

Cement
board

When replacing a tub, allow plenty of
time for wall repair. Removing an old tub
requires removing the wall material at
least 8 inches above the rim of the tub.
For a tiled tub surround like this, you must
fill in the cavity with cement board.

REMOVING A TUB

If your tub is chipped, difficult to keep clean, or just plain ugly, consider refinishing rather than replacing. You'll probably find several companies in the phone book that use various methods. Check out samples of their work and read their guarantees carefully. Note that no refinishing method can produce a finish that is as hard and durable as a new tub.

Plan and prepare
Measure your tub and make sure that you will be able to get it past other fixtures and out the door. You may have to take the door off its hinges. Remove the sink or the toilet if they will be in the way.

A dropcloth is probably not enough protection for the floor. To be safe, cut and tape pieces of plywood to the floor and cover with a dropcloth.

Sometimes old tiles can be removed and reused. However, at least some will probably break. Either find tiles to match or plan to retile the walls. Or install a solid-surface tub surround *(pages 52–53)*.

PRESTART CHECKLIST

☐ **TIME**
  A full day to remove a bathtub

☐ **TOOLS**
  Groove-joint pliers, flat pry bar, crowbar, hammer, drill, screwdriver, utility knife

☐ **SKILLS**
  Basic carpentry skills, dismantling a trap

☐ **PREP**
  Locate access to the tub plumbing in the basement below or in an adjacent room; if necessary, install an access panel (opposite page).

☐ **MATERIALS**
  Plywood and dropcloth to protect the floor

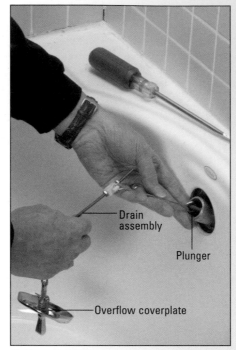

1 From inside the tub, unscrew and remove the overflow coverplate. If a drain assembly is attached to it, pull it out. (A drain assembly with a plunger is shown.) If there is one, unscrew and remove the mounting bracket.

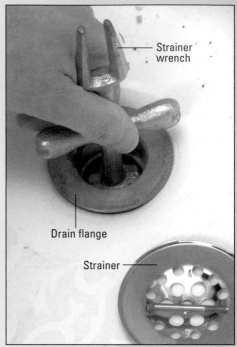

2 To disconnect the drain, you may need to remove a screw or two and remove the strainer. Or you may need to lift out a stopper and a rocker assembly (see *page 50*). Use a strainer wrench to remove the drain flange.

WASTE-AND-OVERFLOW INSTALLATIONS

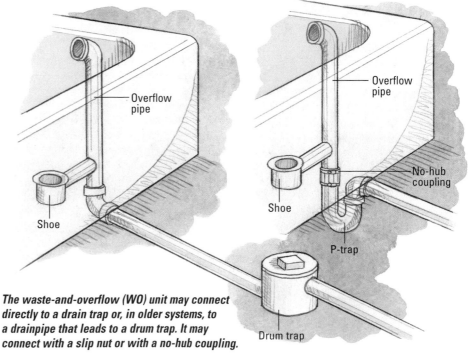

The waste-and-overflow (WO) unit may connect directly to a drain trap or, in older systems, to a drainpipe that leads to a drum trap. It may connect with a slip nut or with a no-hub coupling.

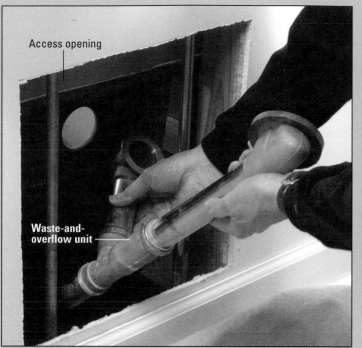

3 From an access panel behind the tub or from below, disconnect the waste-and-overflow (WO) unit from the drain line. Depending on the installation, you may need to unscrew a slip nut or loosen the screws on a no-hub fitting (see *page 50* for alternatives). If the parts are cemented plastic, you'll have to cut through a pipe. Remove the WO unit from the tub. (You may not need to remove the old WO unit if it will fit exactly on the new tub. Measure carefully to be sure.)

4 Remove the tub spout and remove the wall surface all around the tub to a height of about 8 inches. (If there are tub faucet handles, leave them in place if they are at least 8 inches above the tub.) Use a flat pry bar or putty knife to pry off tiles. Cut through drywall with a drywall saw. If the wall is plaster, use a reciprocating saw, taking care not to cut into the studs. Pry off or unscrew nails and screws.

WHAT IF...
You need to install an access panel?

REFRESHER COURSE
Add a ready-made panel

1 If there is no easy access to the plumbing behind the tub, install an access panel in the adjacent room. Use a drywall saw to cut a hole in the wall surface, spanning from stud to stud.

2 Screw 2×2 cleats to either side of the opening. Cut a piece of plywood 2 or 3 inches larger than the opening. Paint it to match the wall and attach it with screws.

Purchase a ready-made plumbing-access panel for a quicker installation and a neater appearance. Follow manufacturer's instructions for cutting the hole and installation.

Removing a tub (continued)

Crowbar

Tub flange

5 Pry out or unscrew any nails or screws anchoring the tub flange to studs. Where the tub rests on the floor, use a utility knife to cut through a bead of caulk, if there is one. Use a crowbar to pry the tub an inch or so away from the back wall.

6 Unless the tub is an old-fashioned clawfoot or other type of stand-alone, it will fit fairly tightly between studs on either side. That means you probably can't slide it outward unless you cut away the wall surface on both sides. The best way is usually to lift the tub up on one end. Pry up one end of the tub first with a crowbar, then with 2×4s. Working with a helper, stand the tub upright.

STANLEY PRO TIP

Removing a cast iron tub

A cast-iron tub weighs 300 to 400 pounds—a bear to remove. If you plan to discard it anyway, break it into manageable pieces. Wear eye protection and gloves. Cover it with an old dropcloth (to prevent pieces from flying) and hit it repeatedly with a sledge hammer.

Choosing a tub

Acrylic or fiberglass tubs are inexpensive, light, and easy to install. Some have finishes that are fairly durable, but they may become dull in time. An enameled steel tub has a sturdier finish but lacks insulating properties; bath water will cool quickly. Enameled cast iron is the most expensive and heaviest material but may be worth the cost because it retains a gleaming finish for decades, fills quietly, and keeps water warm the longest.

Enameled steel

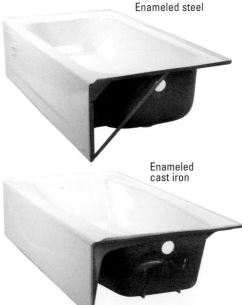

Acrylic

Enameled cast iron

REPLACING A TUB

An inexpensive tub may be narrow and may not cover the the same floor space as the old tub. Many people find a narrow tub uncomfortable. Purchase a tub with ample width.

Home centers carry spa (or whirlpool) tubs that can fit in a standard tub opening. Installing one of these models is not much more work than installing a standard tub; the difference is that a spa or whirlpool needs to plug into a GFCI (Ground Fault Circuit Interrupter) electrical receptacle. For a more elaborate spa installation, see *pages 94–97*.

Preparing the floor and the walls
If the bead of caulk at the base of a tub has even a small gap, water that puddles on the bathroom floor will seep underneath the tub, quickly damaging any bare wood. To be safe, install protective flooring on the entire floor, including the area the tub will cover.

Most tubs fit into a 60-inch opening, but some older ones may be longer. Measure to make sure your replacement tub will fit.

PRESTART CHECKLIST

☐ **TIME**
About a day to install a replacement tub where there is an existing drain

☐ **TOOLS**
Groove-joint pliers, pry bar, level, drill, screwdriver, strainer wrench, putty knife, drill

☐ **SKILLS**
Making drain connections in a tight spot, basic carpentry skills

☐ **PREP**
Clear the area. Cover the floor with plywood and a dropcloth.

☐ **MATERIALS**
Tub, waste-and-overflow unit, plumber's putty, pipe-thread tape, caulk, cement board and tiles, or other wall-finishing material

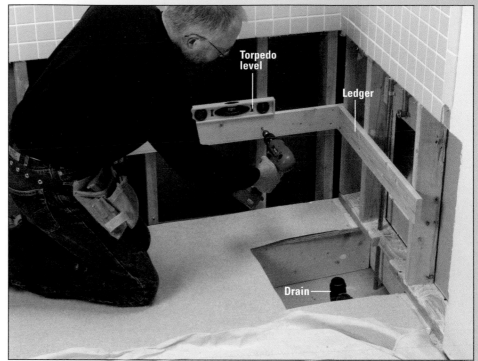

1 Check the drain and replace any damaged parts. Consult the manufacturer's literature and measure to make sure the drain is in the correct location. Purchase a waste-and-overflow unit *(page 50)* and determine how you will connect it to the drain line (see below). Screw ledger boards to the studs at the height recommended by the manufacturer. Ideally, the finish flooring material should run under the tub.

DRAIN CONNECTIONS

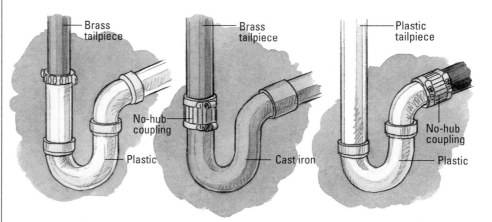

Waste-and-overflow (WO) units have been attached to drain lines in a various ways over the years. Here are some of the most common methods. A rubber no-hub coupling (sometimes called a mission coupling) may be used to connect to a cast-iron or a plastic drain line.

Usually the WO tailpiece connects to the drain via a slip nut. Whichever method you use, plan ahead so that you won't have a nasty surprise after the tub has been wrestled into position.

Replacing a tub (continued)

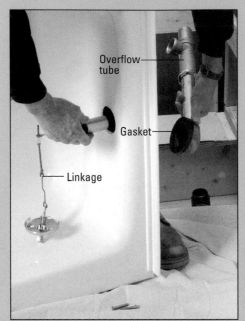

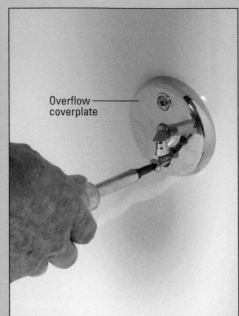

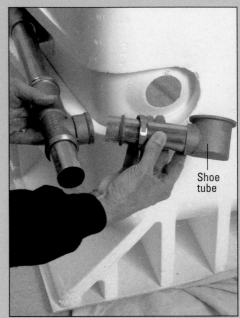

2 Working with the tub turned on its side, dry-fit the overflow tube and the shoe. Make any necessary cuts, then make permanent connections. Place the gasket on the overflow flange, position it behind the overflow hole, and insert the linkage.

3 Inside the tub, slip the screws into the overflow trim. Hold the overflow flange in place and hand-tighten one of the screws. Start the second screw and tighten both with a screwdriver.

4 Insert the shoe tube into the opening in the overflow tube, and slip the other end up into the drain hole.

WHAT IF...
You have an extra-deep tub?

If the tub is deeper than usual, the opening in the overflow tube may be too high for the shoe. If so, cut and install an extension for the overflow tube. In some cases, an extension is included with the waste-and-overflow unit.

BATHTUB WASTE AND OVERFLOW ASSEMBLIES

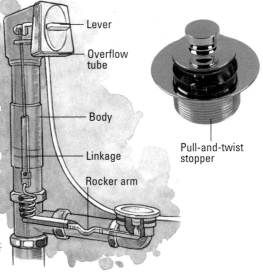

A plunger design has a brass cylinder (or plunger) that slides up and down through the overflow pipe to open or close the drain. A brass pop-up drain has a rocker arm that pivots to raise or lower the stopper.

Many plastic units have no interior mechanism; instead, the stopper itself (above right) is raised and lowered by the bather's toe. This method drains more slowly than the other two methods.

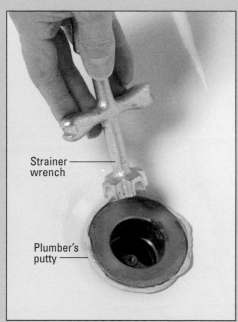

Strainer
wrench

Plumber's
putty

5 Inside the tube, place a rope of plumber's putty under the strainer or drain flange. Hold the shoe with one hand while you screw in the flange. Finish tightening with a strainer wrench. Clean away the squeezed-out putty with a plastic putty knife.

6 Before tilting and moving the tub, plan the move so you avoid damaging the waste-and-overflow unit, which protrudes below the tub. It may work best to rest the tub on 2×4s part of the time. With a helper move the tub into position. You may have to tilt the tub as shown. Slide it into the

opening and gently lower the tub in place. You might want a helper to guide the overflow tube into the drain line (see Step 8) while you do this. Slide the dropcloth or any other protective material out from under the tub. Protect the interior of the tub.

Torpedo
level

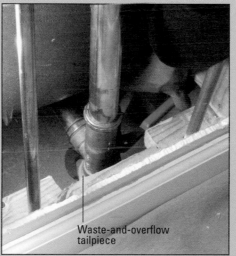

Waste-and-overflow
tailpiece

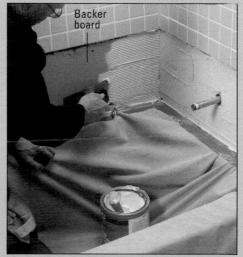

Backer
board

7 Check the tub for level; an out-of-level tub may not drain completely. Attach the tub to the studs according to manufacturer's directions. You will probably nail or screw through an acrylic tub flange (shown). For a metal tub, drive nails just above the flange.

8 Working from behind or below, connect the waste-and-overflow tailpiece to the drain line, using one of the methods shown on *page 49*. To test for leaks, close the stopper and fill the tub. Open the stopper; watch and feel for any sign of wetness.

9 To fill in the gap above the tub, cut and install strips of cement backer board, which is more moisture-resistant than green drywall. Install tiles to fit, allow the adhesive to set for a day, and apply grout. Apply silicone or "tub and tile" caulk where the tiles meet the tub.

INSTALLING A PREFAB TUB SURROUND

A prefab surround is a quick way to give a tub and shower area a fresh start. High-quality units have colorful, durable finishes, as well as convenient niches and towel bars.

Make sure the unit you buy has panels with flanges that overlap each other so you don't have to cut the panels to fit precisely. With a standard 60-inch-wide opening, you probably won't have to cut at all, other than making holes for the spout and the faucet control or handles.

Preparing the wall surface
The walls should be smooth and even. Scrape away any peeling paint and patch any cracks or weak spots. Apply primer paint to the walls to ensure a strong bond with the adhesive. It's possible to install over tile, but the panels will have gaps at the front edges, which must be covered with tile or acrylic.

PRESTART CHECKLIST

☐ **TIME**
Several hours to install a solid-surface tub surround

☐ **TOOLS**
Level, drill, caulk gun (or tube), notched trowel, tape measure, utility knife

☐ **SKILLS**
Measuring and drilling holes

☐ **PREP**
Clean and prime the walls, close the drain and place a dropcloth in the tub, remove the spout and the faucet control or handles.

☐ **MATERIALS**
Shower surround kit, manufacturer's recommended adhesive, masking tape, cardboard for a template

Notched trowel

Center panel

1 Press a corner piece into position and mark the sides and top with a pencil. Using a notched trowel or a caulk gun (depending on the manufacturer), apply adhesive to the area inside the pencil lines. Apply evenly so the panel will not be wavy.

2 Press the center panel in place and smooth it with the butt of your palm. Install other pieces in the same way, following the manufacturer's installation procedures.

PREFAB TUB ENCLOSURE

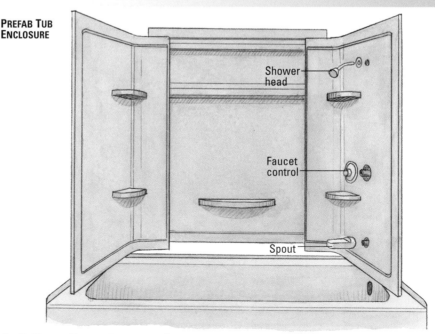

Shower-head

Faucet control

Spout

Available acrylic or polystyrene tub surrounds may have a modern, decorative, or retro look and come in various colors. While these units are less permanent than tile, they install quickly, are relatively inexpensive, and will last for many years.

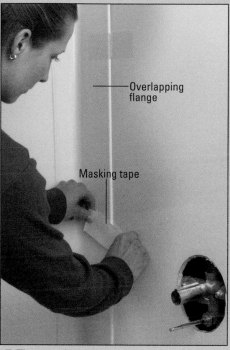

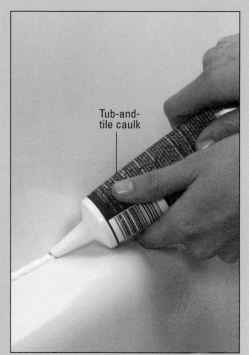

3 Place the piece that will cover the plumbing wall on a scrap piece of plywood. Make a template and cut holes using a utility knife or drill bits and hole saws of the correct size. Install the end pieces in the same way as the back pieces.

4 The panels can be adjusted before the adhesive hardens, which usually occurs about a half hour after application. Apply pieces of masking tape to ensure that their top edges form a straight line. (The bottom edges will be caulked, so they can be slightly uneven.)

5 Apply caulk to the space between the strips and a bead where the panels meet the tub. Practice applying even pressure to the tube while drawing smoothly along the joint. After applying the caulk, smooth it with your finger. Clean up any mistakes with a damp sponge.

Make a template

WHAT IF...
You're installing a shower faucet?

To prevent mistakes in cutting holes, cut a piece of cardboard the same width as the panel to be installed. For each hole, measure up from the tub and over from the corner panel and mark the center of each hole. (If the panel will overlap the corner panel, take that into account.) Cut holes with a utility knife.

Hold the template up against the wall as a trial run. Once you are certain the holes are correct, place the template over the panel and mark it for drilling the holes.

If you need to replace the shower faucet, remove the wall surface. Follow the plumbing instructions on *pages 92–93.* Cover the wall with cement backerboard or water-resistant drywall (greenboard) .

BUILDING A SHOWER ENCLOSURE

A new shower stall installed in a corner of a room will require you to build only one wall. If it's in the middle of a wall, two new walls are required. The walls may reach all the way to the ceiling, or they may stop partway up. In that case the top ledge must be covered with tile or another moisture-resistant surface. The opening can have a door, or you can simply install a curtain rod.

For a corner installation, an integral unit *(page 56)* is much simpler to install, though you have a limited choice of colors.

A 32-inch shower base will feel cramped; buy a base that is at least 34 inches. Some bases must be set in thinset mortar or in a bed of sand, while others can be simply placed on the floor.

For details on how to run drain and supply lines, see "Installing a New Bathroom."

PRESTART CHECKLIST

☐ **TIME**
Two or three days to install a base, plumbing, tiled walls, and a shower door

☐ **TOOLS**
Carpentry tools, groove-joint pliers, drill, tools for plastic and copper pipe *(pages 30–31)*, tiling tools, ¼-inch steel rod

☐ **SKILLS**
Working with plastic and copper pipe, framing a wall, installing tile

☐ **PREP**
Install a drainpipe with trap in the center of the base, as well as supply pipes, faucet, and shower riser.

☐ **MATERIALS**
Shower base, roofing felt, PVC primer and cement, 2×4 studs, cement backer board, backer board screws, tiles, tile adhesive, grout, caulk, shower door

BUILDING A TILED SHOWER ENCLOSURE

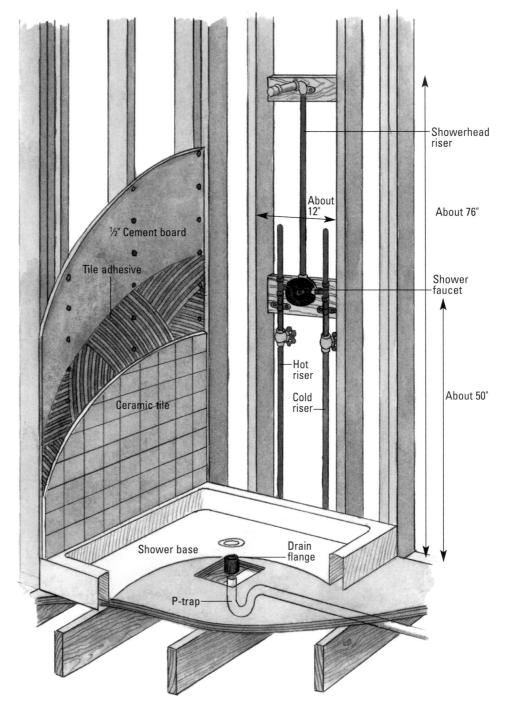

A shower drain should be installed at the center of the shower base. The flange should be level with the floor. Run the supply pipes after the framing is installed.

A. Installing the shower base

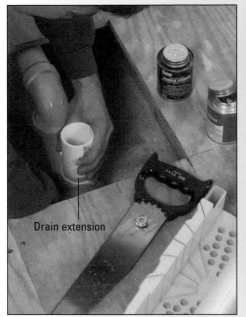

Drain extension

Carpenter's level

Roofing felt

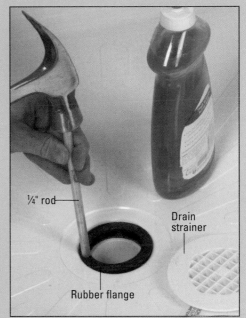

¼" rod

Drain strainer

Rubber flange

1 Set the shower base over the drain to make sure the drain is directly below the opening of the base. Remove the base, cut and cement an extension to the drainpipe. The extension should be flush with the floor.

2 Place a layer or two of roofing felt to smooth any unevenness in the floor. (Some manufacturers may require a bed of mortar or sand.) Set the shower base over the drain to confirm that the drain is positioned where you want it. Check for level; shim with roofing felt as needed.

3 Using liquid soap as a lubricant, fit the rubber flange (provided with the shower base) over the drain extension and push it as far down as you can. Tap it all the way in place with a ¼-inch rod. Install the drain strainer.

REFRESHER COURSE
Installing a drain

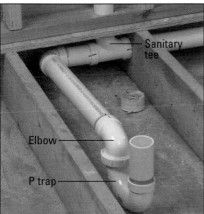

Sanitary tee

Elbow

P trap

See *pages 84–87* for instructions on running a new drain line. A shower drain should be connected directly to a trap. Drain lines must slope at a rate of ¼ inch per running foot and must be properly vented (see *pages 10–11*).

WHAT IF...
The base uses a PVC flange?

Strainer

Drain body

Fiber gasket

Rubber gasket

Drain flange

Cement the drain flange to the drainpipe; the flange should be flush with the floor. Set the gaskets on top of the flange. Place the shower base over the drain hole. Check that the gaskets are still in place. Screw the drain body through the hole in the base and into the flange. Attach the strainer.

STANLEY PRO TIP

Hire a pro when installing a mortar-laid shower base

A mortar-laid, tiled shower base can be customized to whatever style, size, and color you want. With it you can achieve a truly custom look. However, it is a major project in itself, requiring substantial prep work, including the services of a professional plumber.

Once the base of the shower is framed, a plumber should install the drain and join it to the CPE (heavy plastic) liner set inside the frame. A drain flange must be installed precisely so that water cannot seep under the liner. Then the area around the drain is filled with mortar, shaped so it slopes down toward the drain. When the mortar sets, tiles are installed on top.

B. Framing the shower

2×4 stud wall

Doubled 2×4 stud at outside corners

Protect base with a dropcloth

Cement backer board

1 With the shower base in place, build 2×4 walls for the sides. Remember that the studs will be covered with ½-inch-thick cement board, plus the tiles (usually about ⅜ inch thick). No studs should be farther apart than 16 inches. On the plumbing wall, space the studs so you can position the shower faucet—a pair of studs spaced about a foot apart will accommodate most faucets. Install horizontal braces to support both the faucet and the shower head arm. Some bases may require a ledger *(page 49)*. Install the supply pipes and faucet, following instructions on *pages 92–93*.

2 Cut pieces of cement backer board to fit. Cover all wood surfaces with the backer board. Attach them to the studs with backer board screws. Check that the wall surface is smooth and even because the tiles will follow any contours. Before tiling, fill the gap at the bottom with caulk.

Available shower units

Corner and rectangular shower stalls—made of acrylic fiberglass or polystyrene— are much easier to install than a custom-made enclosure. One-piece units are designed for new construction only because they are too large to fit through a door. Three-piece units are quickly assembled and are ideal for remodeling.

Two or three walls of these units must be installed up against solid walls. A corner unit can simply be installed in any corner that is reasonably square. A rectangular or square unit requires an opening of the correct width and height.

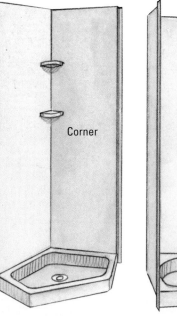

Corner

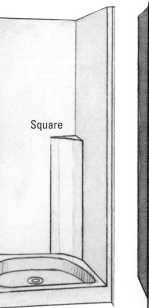

Square

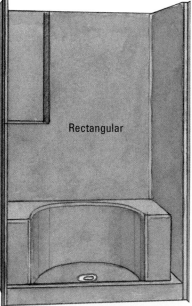

Rectangular

Ceramic tile

Grout float

3 Cover the backer board with ceramic tile or with a shower enclosure kit (see *pages 52–53*). Consult a book on tiling for guidelines on selecting, laying out, and cutting tile. In general tiling should be planned to minimize small pieces. Wherever a tile edge will be exposed, install a bullnose piece, which has one finished edge (see illustration below). Use a notched trowel to apply thinset mortar or organic tile adhesive and set the tiles. Use a tile-cutting hole saw for the faucet and shower head stubouts.

Once all the tiles are applied, allow the adhesive to set overnight.

4 Mix a batch of latex-reinforced grout and use a grout float to first push the grout into the joints and then scrape away most of the excess. Wipe several times with a damp sponge, working to create consistent grout lines. Allow to dry, and buff with a dry towel. Caulk all the inside corners.

Caulk the edges of the stall

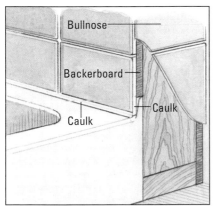

Bullnose

Backerboard

Caulk

Caulk

The bottom of a wall, where the tiles meet the shower base, must be installed correctly or water will seep behind the tiles and damage the studs. Install the backer board to the top of the base's flange and fill the gap below with caulk. Apply tiles and apply a bead of caulk.

Installing a shower door

Jamb piece

Measure the opening and select a door with a frame you can adjust to fit your unit. Follow manufacturer's instructions. In general, you'll begin by cutting the jamb piece to size and installing a bottom track and seal. Each jamb is made of two interlocking pieces. One attaches

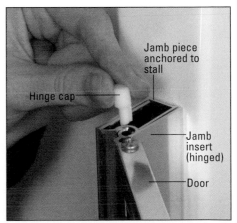

Jamb piece anchored to stall

Hinge cap

Jamb insert (hinged)

Door

to the stall with screws and anchors. When both jambs are installed, decide which way the door should swing and install the hinged insert with the clamps provided. Slide the door in place, cap, and add the door handle. Install the other jamb insert and adjust.

SYSTEM REPAIRS & UPGRADES

Home plumbing systems periodically need maintenance and appliance upgrades. These chores are moderately difficult—more involved than "easy installs" but not as complicated as a bathroom or kitchen renovation. Some projects may call for running short lengths of new supply pipe or gas pipe but no elaborate drain-waste-vent installations.

Some building inspectors will want you to obtain a permit for any installation, no matter how small. Others don't want to conduct inspections unless an installation requires running new pipes. To be safe consult with your local building department before tackling any of the projects described in this chapter.

An inspector may provide valuable advice for some of the more complicated connections, such as connecting water, gas, or electric lines to a water heater *(pages 60–63)* or solving water pressure problems *(pages 68–69)*.

Other sources of advice and help

If you have a gas water heater, call the gas company to check for gas leaks and carbon monoxide (which can build up dangerously if the flue is not installed correctly). They may perform these checks for free.

If your main drain line is clogged, have the city inspect its portion of the drain line; again, this should be free.

If you have an old home or if your plumbing is too complicated for you to understand, do not hesitate to call a plumber. Their hourly rates may be expensive; but pros can perform some tasks so quickly that it may be well worth the money to hire them.

These maintenance and upgrade projects are straightforward and can be done in a weekend.

CHAPTER PREVIEW

Repairing a gas water heater
page 60

Repairing electric water heater
page 62

Replacing a water heater
page 64

Increasing water pressure
page 68

Shut off water before draining.

Pressure-relief valve

SAFETY FIRST
Shut down water
heater before draining

Always turn off the water heater before draining. With an electric water heater (shown), shut off electric power at the breaker box *(page 62)*. With a gas unit, shut off gas at the burner control unit *(page 61)*.

If water in your area is mineral-laden, draining the water heater once a year will prolong its life. Shut off the water and the gas or electricity before draining. Once the water has drained, close the drain valve, turn on the water, and wait for the unit to fill before restoring gas or electric power.

Use a hose to run water to a floor drain or use a bucket, shutting off the drain valve with each filling.

Drain valve

Installing a
water filter
page 70

Installing a
hose bib
page 72

Clearing drain
lines
page 74

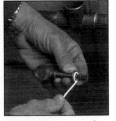

Replacing a valve
page 76

REPAIRING A GAS WATER HEATER

Most repairs to a gas water heater are made at the burner control. If your heater leaks, the tank is rusted through and the entire unit must be replaced *(pages 64–65)*. Here's a quick troubleshooting guide to gas water heater problems:

■ If the unit suddenly stops heating water, try relighting the pilot. If it does not stay lit, the thermocouple probably needs to be replaced *(right)*. If that does not solve the problem, you may need to clean the burner.

■ If the flame is mostly yellow rather than mostly blue, clean the burner.

■ If water isn't heating sufficiently even though the thermostat is turned up and the flames are blue, drain the tank and refill it *(page 59)*.

■ If you have hard water, unscrew and remove the anode rod once a year. Look for a 1-inch nut in the top of the heater. Loosen the nut: The anode rod will be attached. If it's encrusted with minerals, replace it to get more efficient operation.

PRESTART CHECKLIST

☐ **TIME**
About an hour to replace a thermocouple; two to three hours to service a burner

☐ **TOOLS**
Long matches or a barbecue lighter, screwdriver, adjustable wrench, groove-joint pliers, thin wire, soft metal brush

☐ **SKILLS**
No special skills are needed.

☐ **PREP**
Clear the area. You may need to shut off the gas.

☐ **MATERIALS**
New thermocouple of the correct length, new pressure-relief valve

A. Replacing a thermocouple

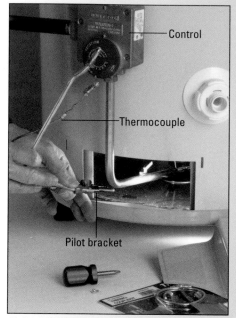

Control

Thermocouple

Pilot bracket

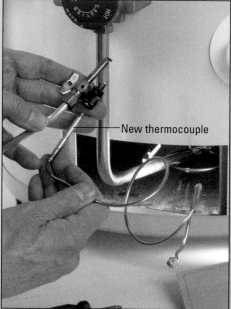

New thermocouple

1 If a pilot light won't stay lit after you've followed the lighting directions, **turn the gas-control knob to OFF.** It's often easiest to detach the thermocouple and pilot supply tube at the control and, using a stubby screwdriver, disconnect them from the burner. Pull out the thermocouple.

2 Purchase a thermocouple the same length as the old one. Unroll it carefully to avoid kinking. Insert the tip into the pilot bracket so the pilot flame will heat it. Reinstall the thermocouple and the supply tube and attach them at the control. Turn the gas back on and light the pilot.

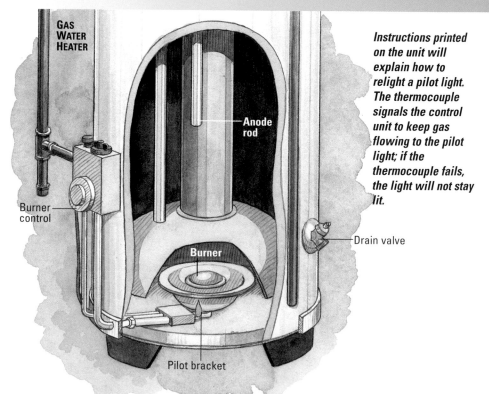

GAS WATER HEATER

Anode rod

Burner control

Burner

Pilot bracket

Drain valve

Instructions printed on the unit will explain how to relight a pilot light. The thermocouple signals the control unit to keep gas flowing to the pilot light; if the thermocouple fails, the light will not stay lit.

B. Servicing a burner

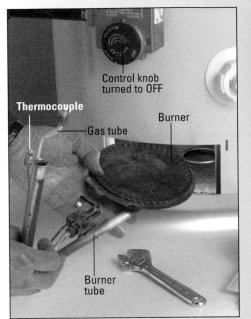

Control knob turned to OFF

Thermocouple

Gas tube

Burner

Burner tube

1 If flames are yellow or erratic, remove and clean the burner. **Turn the gas control knob to OFF.** Unscrew and pull the gas tube, burner tube, and thermocouple from the control. Reach inside the chamber and pull the burner unit out or down until it unclips. Carefully pull the unit out.

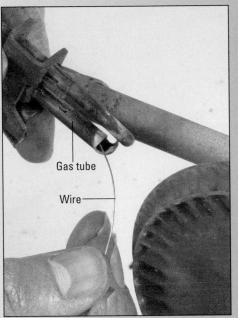

Gas tube

Wire

2 Unscrew the burner unit from the gas tube. Clean the pilot gas tube with a soft wire brush or poke a thin wire down into its hole.

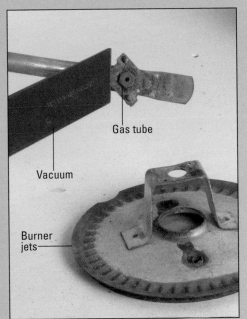

Gas tube

Vacuum

Burner jets

3 Turn the burner upside down and shake out any debris. Vacuum the jets to remove all dust. Use a thin wire to make sure the opening in the gas tube is clear and vacuum out any debris. Reassemble, reinstall, and relight. If the burner still malfunctions, call for service.

SAFETY FIRST
Check the flue

The flue on a gas water heater should pull all fumes up and send them out of the house. To check that a flue is working, light a match, blow it out, and hold it near the flue. Smoke should be sucked up into the flue. If it isn't, check that all the connections are tight. Have the gas company inspect to be sure.

Maintaining a gas water heater

Keep your heater alive longer by following these tips:

■ In areas with hard water, a gas water heater will last no more than 10 years. If you drain the unit once a year (see *page 59*), you will not only lengthen the unit's life but also increase its efficiency.

■ The higher a thermostat is set, the shorter the life of the water heater. Set the temperature to just as hot as you want and no higher.

■ A damaged or incorrectly installed flue will lead to elevated levels of carbon-monoxide. Install a carbon-monoxide detector near (or directly above) the water heater to warn of this dangerous gas.

■ New water heaters are well insulated, but an older unit will benefit from a slip-over insulation blanket made for water heaters.

Pressure-relief valve

A temperature-and-pressure-relief valve is a safety device that provides an outlet for water in case the unit overheats. To test that it's working, pull up on the little lever; water should flow out. If not, or if water drips from the valve, install a replacement.

REPAIRING AN ELECTRIC WATER HEATER

Most repairs to an electric water heater are made at the two elements, each of which has a thermostat. If water leaks onto the floor, the tank is rusted through, and the entire unit must be replaced *(pages 64–67)*.

■ If water is not hot enough, try turning up the thermostat settings for both elements.

■ If the unit suddenly stops heating water, press the reset button, usually located on the high-limit cutoff. If you hear a click, the unit is reset and the problem may be solved. Also check that power is reaching the unit; call in an electrician if you are not sure.

■ If water gets warm but not hot, replace the upper element and/or thermostat.

■ If water gets hot, but the hot water runs out quicker than it used to, replace the lower element and/or thermostat.

■ If the unit is noisy, drain the tank and refill it. If that does not solve the problem, remove and clean the elements.

■ If water is too hot even with the thermostats turned down, replace either the thermostat or the high-limit cutoff.

PRESTART CHECKLIST

☐ **TIME**
An hour or two for most repairs

☐ **TOOLS**
Voltage tester, groove-joint pliers, screwdriver

☐ **SKILLS**
Testing for electrical power, unscrewing and replacing devices

☐ **PREP**
Prepare the household for doing without hot water for a few hours. Arrange for a work light while the power is off.

☐ **MATERIALS**
New element, thermostat, or high-limit cutoff for your make and model of water heater

Circuit breaker

1 The amount of power an electric water heater uses is dangerous. Check with an electrician if you are unsure about shutting off power. At the service panel, **shut off the breaker or unscrew the fuse controlling the water heater. Be sure no one will turn power on while you work.**

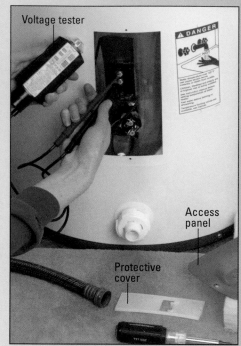

Voltage tester

Access panel

Protective cover

2 Close the water shutoff valve above the tank. Drain the tank *(page 59).* Remove the access panel and the protective cover. Press the two prongs of a voltage tester against the terminal screws that the wires are connected to; test all possible combinations. Be certain that power is off.

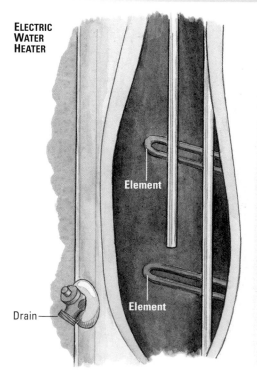

ELECTRIC WATER HEATER

Element

Element

Drain

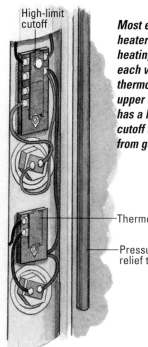

High-limit cutoff

Thermostat

Pressure-relief tube

Most electric water heaters have two heating elements, each with its own thermostat. The upper element also has a high-limit cutoff to keep water from getting too hot.

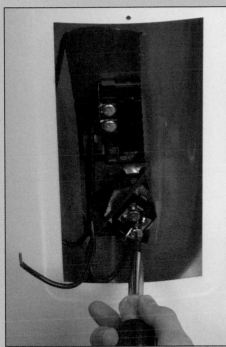

Element

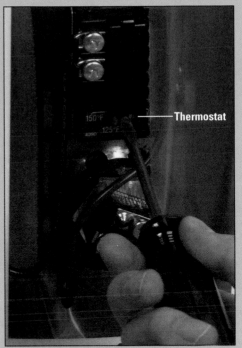
Thermostat

3 Loosen the element's terminal screws and pull the wires away. You don't need to mark the wires—they can be attached to either terminal.

4 Use groove-joint pliers to loosen and unscrew the element. Pull out the element. Have an appliance parts dealer test the element and buy a duplicate if it's defective. If the element is working, try replacing the thermostat.

5 Scrape away any debris from around the opening, then clean it with a rag. Screw in the new element, replace the wires, replace the cover, and refill the tank. Set the thermostat (see *below*), restore power, and test.

replacing the thermostat.

WHAT IF ...
A high-limit cutoff is defective?

High-limit cutoff

If water overheats or if the unit does not heat water and other solutions do not solve the problem, remove the high-limit cutoff and take it in for testing. Replace it if necessary.

Replacing the thermostat

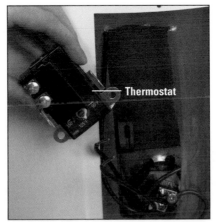
Thermostat

To remove a thermostat, shut off power and test that power is off. Disconnect and tag the wires. Remove any mounting nuts or screws and pry out the thermostat. Have the thermostat tested and replace it if necessary.

Resetting and adjusting a thermostat

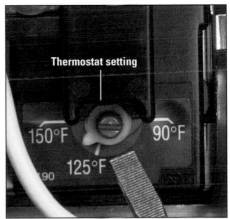
Thermostat setting
150°F   90°F
125°F

A water heater is commonly set to 120 degrees. If water seems too hot or too cold, adjust the temperature up or down by about 10 degrees. After a day of use, you may want to adjust it another 10 degrees.

REPLACING A WATER HEATER

This job may seem complicated, but it's actually straightforward. If the new unit is the same size as the old one and has connections located in the same places, hooking up the water, the gas, and the flue will be simple. If you need to move any of those lines, the job will take a few more hours.

There should be a shutoff valve for the cold water pipe that enters the water heater (do not add one to the exiting hot water line), and for the gas line as well. If any valves are lacking, install them when you install the new water heater.

If you live in an area that experiences earthquakes, local codes may require that you chain or strap the water heater firmly to a wall.

Arrange for disposal of the old water heater. Your local waste hauler may have special requirements.

PRESTART CHECKLIST

☐ **TIME**
About a day for most installations

☐ **TOOLS**
Groove-joint pliers, screwdriver, pipe wrenches, adjustable wrench, tools for cutting and joining steel and/or copper pipe, two-wheeled cart, torpedo level, hammer

☐ **SKILLS**
Assembling supply pipe and gas pipe, maneuvering and leveling a large appliance, working with a flue

☐ **PREP**
Clear a path for removing the old unit; prepare the household to be without hot water for a day; check local codes.

☐ **MATERIALS**
New gas water heater, shims, gas pipe or flexible connector, water pipe and/or flexible connector, heat trap nipples, pipe-thread tape, flue extension (optional), pressure-relief valve

Installing a gas water heater

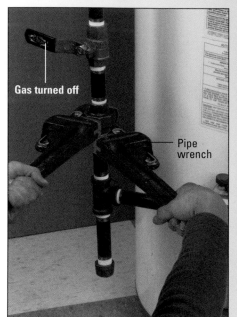

1 **Turn off the gas shutoff valve** (so the handle is perpendicular to the pipe). **Shut off water** and allow the tank to cool. Drain the tank *(page 59).* If there is a gas pipe union, use two pipe wrenches to disconnect it. If there is a flexible fitting (see Step 8, *page 66),* disconnect it.

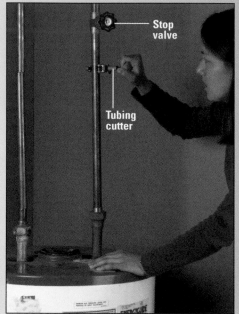

2 Disconnect the water lines. If there is no flexible connector or union to disconnect, you may have to cut through a solid copper pipe. Use a tubing cutter to make a clean cut so you can connect the new line to it.

3 Once the flue has cooled, detach it from the water heater. Tie the flue up to keep it out of the way. With a two-wheeled cart, remove the old unit. Mineral deposits make it heavier than a new unit.

4 Carry or wheel in the new water heater. Position it so the water, gas, and flue connections are as easy to reach as possible. Use a level to check the unit for plumb and shim the legs if necessary.

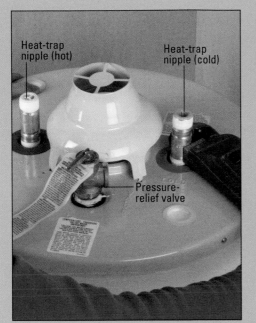

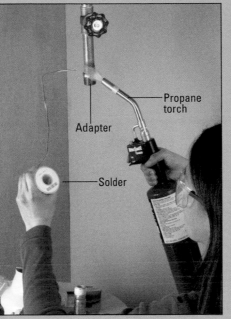

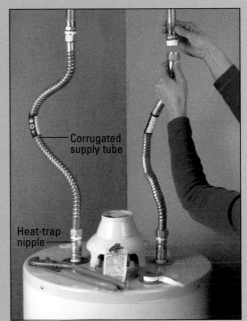

5 Install heat-trap nipples to the water heater inlets. Install the blue nipple, its arrow pointing down, to the cold water inlet. Install the red nipple, its arrow pointing up, to the hot-water inlet. Tighten both with a pipe wrench. Run PVC from the pressure-relief valve to a floor drain *(page 67)*.

6 Before hooking up the supply lines, you may need to install an adapter. For a copper pipe that has been cut, sweat a male adapter to each pipe.

7 Connect the water supply tubes to the heat-trap nipples. Buy connectors approved by local codes, checking that they fit at both ends. If necessary, use reducer fittings to make the transition.

Flexible water connectors

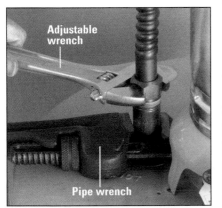

If flexible water lines attach to the old water heater, simply unscrew the nuts with an adjustable wrench to disconnect. Check that the old fittings will work with the new; you may need to buy new lines or a male or female adapter. Check local codes.

Choosing a water heater

Different water heaters serve different needs. When shopping for a new unit consider the following:
■ Check the energy guide sticker on a water heater and choose one that's well insulated. Though it may cost a bit more, it will save money in the long run.
■ If family members complain that water runs out during showers, consider buying a unit with an additional 10 gallons of capacity. It may take more time to install and will use a little more energy.
■ Check the "rate of recovery"—how quickly the unit heats water. A water heater with a quick rate of recovery may solve the problem of running out of hot water.
■ If you have hard water, consider a unit with two anode rods, which attract sediment. Regularly cleaning the rods can add years to the life of a water heater.

Buy connectors approved by local codes

Choosing connectors
Local codes may have specific requirements for the type of pipe or connectors to be used when hooking up a water heater.

Unlike a range, a water heater usually is not moved during its life. However, it may vibrate while in use. Some building departments prefer flexible connectors, while others prefer hard piping—both for the water supplies and for the gas line. Always follow local codes.

If there is no floor drain nearby, you may want to place a drain pan under the water heater to catch water in case of a small leak.

Installing a gas water heater (continued)

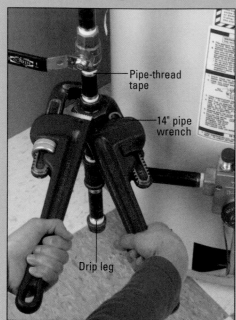

Pipe-thread tape

14" pipe wrench

Drip leg

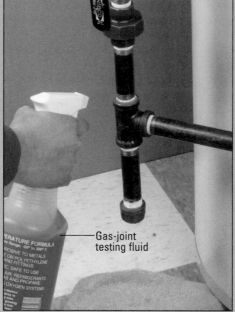

Gas-joint testing fluid

Reset button

8 Connect the gas line. A hard-piped gas line should have a drip leg to collect condensation and dirt that can hinder the burner's efficiency. Wrap the pipe threads with yellow pipe-thread tape (made for gas lines). Tighten connections securely using two pipe wrenches (see *pages 36–37*).

9 Do not light the pilot until you are sure there are no leaks. Turn on the gas. Test for leaks by spraying with gas-joint testing fluid (shown) or by pouring a strong soap-and-water mixture on each joint. Bubbles indicate a leak. Tighten leaky fittings. Recheck, if necessary.

10 Follow manufacturer's instructions for lighting the pilot. Usually this involves lighting the pilot while holding down the reset button and continuing to hold it for a full minute before releasing and turning on the burner.

CONNECT THE GAS LINE
Use a flexible connector

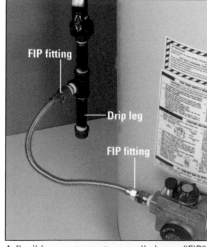

FIP fitting

Drip leg

FIP fitting

A flexible gas connector usually has a "FIP" fitting at each end. For the best burner performance, install a drip leg as shown.

Attaching a flue

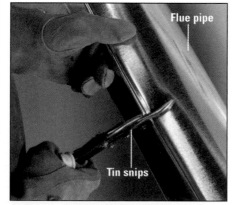

Flue pipe

Tin snips

Sheet-metal screw

1 If the new heater is the same height as the old water heater, you can simply hook up the flue in the same way. If you need to add piping, measure and cut pieces to fit with a pair of tin snips.

2 Connect the pieces by driving three or four sheet-metal screws into each joint. Test to make sure the flue draws *(page 61)* and install a carbon-monoxide detector in the room. If you have any doubts about the flue, have the gas company or a plumbing and heating contractor inspect it.

Installing an electric water heater

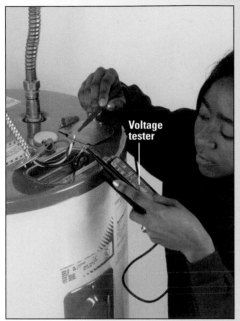

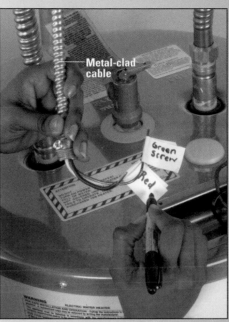

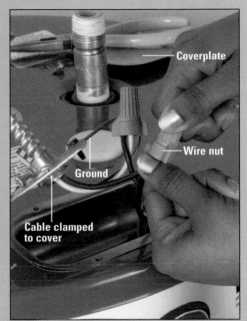

1 To replace an electric water heater, **shut off power** (see *page 62*). Test to make sure power is off. Remove the electrical coverplate and carefully pull out the wires; remove the wire nuts and touch the bare wires with the probes of a voltage tester.

2 Once you are sure power is off, loosen the cable clamp screw and pull out the cable, which might be metal-clad (shown), non-metallic cable, or wires running through conduit. Mark the wires for reattaching. Follow steps on *page 64* to disconnect the water lines and remove the old unit.

3 Position the new unit, level it, and shim if needed. Run the electrical cable through the clamp and tighten it. Connect the ground wire to the ground screw. Splice the other wires and screw on wire nuts. Push the wires into the cavity and replace the coverplate.

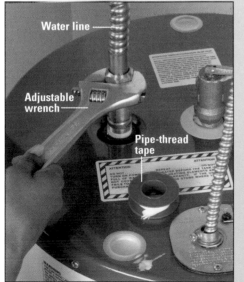

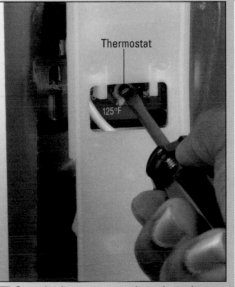

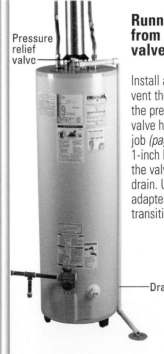

4 Install the water lines (see *page 65*). Open the water shutoff valves and allow the tank to fill. Do not restore power yet.

5 Open both access panels and set the thermostats to the desired settings. Press the reset buttons until they click. Restore power.

Running a line from a relief valve to a drain

Install a drain tube to vent the water should the pressure relief valve have to do its job *(page 61)*. Run a 1-inch PVC line from the valve to a floor drain. Use a PVC adapter to make the transition.

INCREASING WATER PRESSURE

If you have low water pressure, first check that water arrives to your home at 40–100 pounds per square inch (psi). If the incoming pressure is within that range but you have galvanized-steel pipes, sediment or mineral buildup may be the problem. Hot-water pipes are more prone to clogs than cold-water pipes. Horizontal pipes collect more sediment than vertical pipes. However, any galvanized pipe can clog.

The ultimate solution is to replace old plumbing with copper pipes—a time-consuming and expensive job. Here are several partial solutions that are more easily accomplished. The method shown at right is a proven way to clear pipes but can also reveal corroded joints where built-up sediment alone was keeping leaks from happening. **Use compressed air gently.** Clear pipes between a faucet and the water heater, then use the same method to clear pipes from the water heater to the main shutoff. Avoid blasting compressed air through a water heater—you could damage its lining.

PRESTART CHECKLIST

☐ **TIME**
Several hours to assemble the parts and force out sediment with an air compressor

☐ **TOOLS**
Pipe wrenches, groove-joint pliers, air compressor, hand-crank auger, wire cutters, electrician's fish tape

☐ **SKILLS**
Dismantling and assembling galvanized-steel pipe

☐ **PREP**
Determine which pipes are clogged and map where the pipes run (see *pages 20–21*).

☐ **MATERIALS**
Parts to connect an air compressor to a pipe, pipe-thread tape, pan or bucket

Forcing out sediment with an air compressor

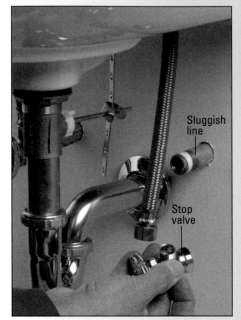

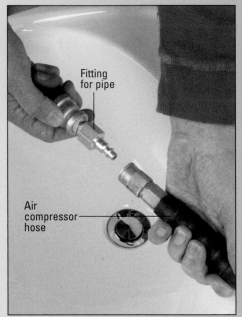

1 Shut off the clogged supply line at a convenient spot on the street side of a union (see Step 3). At the other end of the pipe run to be cleared, disconnect pipes or remove a stop valve.

2 Attach the hose of an air compressor (a model that has a holding tank) to the pipe end. Making this connection requires several fittings; consult with a home center salesperson to assemble them properly.

Clearing aerators and screens

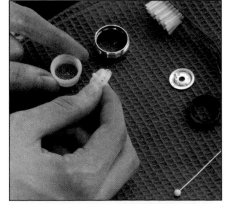

If water flows slowly at one faucet or appliance only, chances are that an aerator or a screen is clogged. At a washing machine, shut off the hose valve and disconnect the hoses from the back of the machine. Pry out the screens located either in the machine's inlets or in the hose ends and clean them.

Use pliers to unscrew an aerator from the end of a faucet spout and clean all the little parts. Replace the aerator if it is damaged.

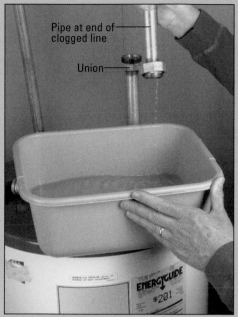

Pipe at end of clogged line

Union

3 While you are at the compressor, have a helper disconnect the union on the house side of the shutoff valve, such as a union near a water heater (shown). Place a pan or bucket under the union. Water contained in the pipes will flow out.

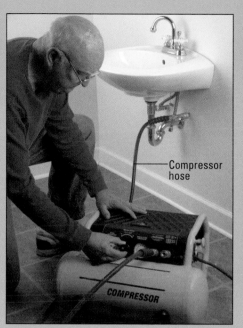

Compressor hose

COMPRESSOR

4 As soon as the union is disconnected, turn on the compressor. Water—along with a good deal of gunk—will gush out the pipe at the other end. Repeat this process once or twice to force out lingering sediment.

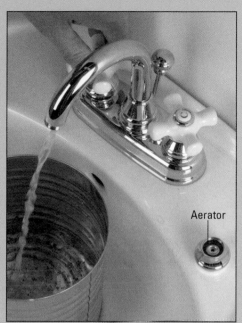

Aerator

5 Reattach the union and the pipe or stop valve to the other end and turn on the water. Remove the aerators from all affected faucets and run water for a minute or two to flush out more sediment.

Augering supply pipes

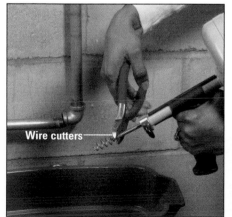

Wire cutters

1 To ream out a pipe, buy an inexpensive hand-crank auger and cut off its tip with a pair of wire cutters so it can fit into a clogged pipe. The resulting tool will run through straight sections of pipe only. **Shut off the water** and drain the line.

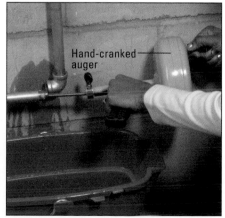

Hand-cranked auger

2 Disassemble the pipe at both ends. Push the auger through, turning the crank if necessary. Pull the auger out and flush the pipe with running water.

STANLEY PRO TIP

Replacing pipes

If water runs slowly throughout the house, replacing a few of the first pipes that enter the house may help substantially. If these pipes are exposed in a basement or crawlspace, replacing them will not be difficult.

Start as near to the street as possible and remove all the pipes—both horizontals and verticals—that you can easily reach. Before installing the new pipes, use a hose to run water backward through the pipes that you did not remove. If you will install copper pipe, connect it to a galvanized pipe with a dielectric union *(page 24)*.

If a single faucet is sluggish, you may be able to remove and replace the short pipe (usually horizontal) to which the stop valve is attached. Often this pipe is clogged, and you'll see significant improvement when you replace it.

INSTALLING A WATER FILTER

Water from a public utility must meet strict health requirements. If you have reason to think that your water is unsafe (for instance, if it's from a private well), have it tested by a local health department, the utility company, or an extension office of a state university.

Even the safest water may be distasteful and even smelly, and it may produce stains. A filter could be the solution.

If chlorine is the cause of bad taste, a temporary solution is to run water into a pitcher and let it sit in the refrigerator overnight. By morning much of the chlorine will have leached out, often making the water palatable.

When to add a water softener

Hard water—water laden with minerals—can hinder the lathering action of detergent, making it difficult to clean clothes. Hard water may also stain fixtures and ceramic tiles and clog pipes. A water softener uses an ionization process to solve these problems. It also can remove rust from water.

PRESTART CHECKLIST

☐ **TIME**
An hour or two to install a whole-house filter

☐ **TOOLS**
Tools for working with copper or galvanized pipe, groove-joint pliers, canister wrench

☐ **SKILLS**
Working with copper or galvanized supply pipe

☐ **PREP**
Find a convenient location to install the filter so that you can change cartridges easily.

☐ **MATERIALS**
Water filter, pipe adapters, shutoff valve, perhaps a jumper wire with clamps

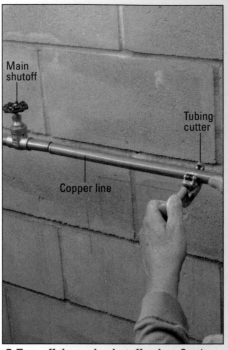

Main shutoff

Copper line

Tubing cutter

1 **Turn off the main shutoff valve.** On the house side of the main shutoff, break into the supply line. If the pipes are galvanized, find a union or cut with a hacksaw and install a union *(pages 36–37)*. Cut into a copper line using a tubing cutter.

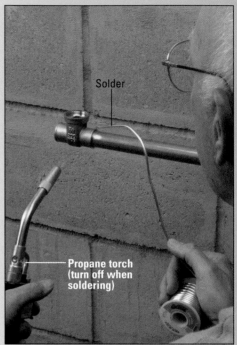

Solder

Propane torch (turn off when soldering)

2 Install a ball or gate shutoff valve on the house side of the water filter. Remove the insides of the valve before sweating the valve body in place. (Some plumbers like to install a bypass loop with additional stop valves so water can be rerouted should the entire filter unit need replacing.)

PROBLEM-SOLVING FILTERS

A plumbing inspector or local contractor should know which type of filter works best for the water in your area. Here are some qualities of the most popular filter types.

Problem	Solution
Soap does not lather well; soap scum residue on clothes and fixtures	Water softener
Rust stains	Water softener or charcoal filter
Rotten-egg smell due to high sulphur content	Oxidizing filter or a chlorinization feeder system
Chlorine odor and taste	Carbon filter
Water appears cloudy or dirty	Particle filter
Harmful bacteria or chemicals suspected	Reverse-osmosis filter

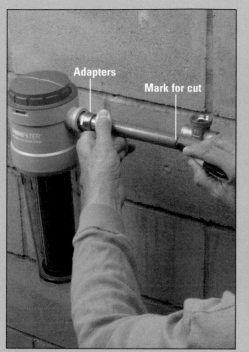

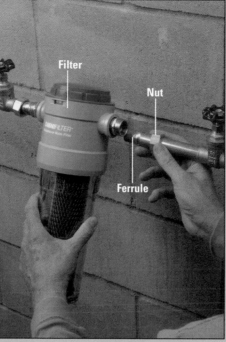

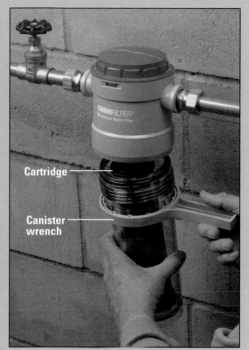

3 Purchase the adapters you need to connect the filter to your size and type of pipe. (These parts may come in a kit, but be sure they fit your pipes.) Install the adapters on either side of the filter. Hold the filter in place and measure for cutting the pipe that emerges from the new shutoff valve.

4 Slide nuts and ferrules onto the pipes on either side. Slip the filter onto the pipes, slide the ferrules and nuts over to the filter, and tighten the nuts.

5 Place a filter cartridge in the canister and twist the canister onto the filter unit. Tighten with a special canister wrench.

SAFETY FIRST
Jumper wire for grounding

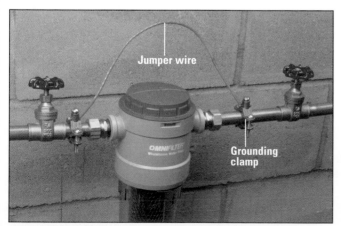

If the electrical system is grounded via the cold-water pipe, adding a water filter will interrupt the path to the ground, leaving all your electricity ungrounded. Install a jumper wire using approved grounding clamps.

REFRESHER COURSE
Under-sink filters

If your main concern is the quality of your drinking water, there's no need to filter all the water entering the house. Install a small filter under the kitchen sink and hook it to the cold water. A unit like this can be installed simply by connecting tubes to the stop valve and to the faucet.

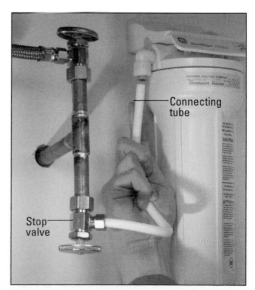

INSTALLING A HOSE BIB

A conveniently located hose bib (sometimes called a "sill cock") can save you from having to stretch a garden hose around the house. The most difficult part of installing a hose is breaking into a cold-water supply pipe and installing a tee fitting. The type shown has an extended stem so that the freeze-sensitive valve is indoors. Instructions on these pages include installing a shutoff valve so you can turn water off from the inside as well as the outside.

Choosing a hose bib

If you live in an area with freezing winters and the hose bib pipe will enter a heated room, buy a long-stemmed, frost-free sill cock (as shown at right), which shuts water off inside rather than outside. If you live in a warm climate, simply connect pipe to a standard hose bib.

If the hose bib will attach to a sprinkler system, install a hose bib with an anti-siphon device, which prevents water from backing up into the house and possibly contaminating your household water.

PRESTART CHECKLIST

☐ **TIME**
An hour or two to tap into a supply line and install a hose bib

☐ **TOOLS**
Tools for working with copper or galvanized pipe, carpenter's square, drill, drill bit, screwdriver, caulk gun

☐ **SKILLS**
Working with supply pipe

☐ **PREP**
Find a location that's convenient for attaching hoses and close to a cold-water pipe.

☐ **MATERIALS**
Hose bib, deck screws, silicone caulk, pipe and fittings, pipe-thread tape

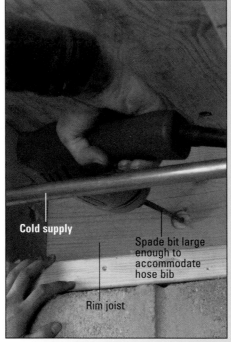

Cold supply

Spade bit large enough to accommodate hose bib

Rim joist

1 At a point slightly higher than the cold-water pipe you will tap into, drill a finder hole with a long, thin bit *(page 107)*. Bore through the rim joist, sheathing, and siding. To avoid splintering the wood, drill part way from the indoors out, then finish by drilling from the outside in.

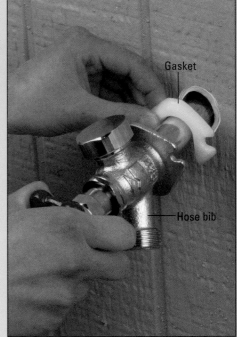

Gasket

Hose bib

2 From the outside, slip on the plastic gasket and push the hose bib through the hole. Apply silicone caulk around the hole and attach the hose bib by driving two deck screws that are coated to resist rusting.

FROST-FREE HOSE BIB INSTALLATION

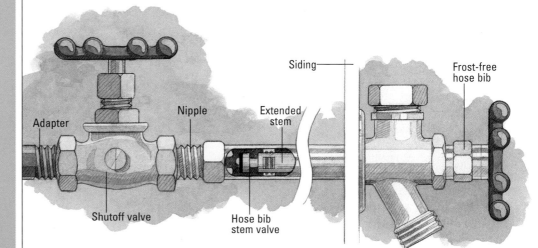

Adapter

Shutoff valve

Nipple

Hose bib stem valve

Siding

Extended stem

Frost-free hose bib

Plan for all the pieces you will need to install a hose bib. In this case, a short nipple connects the hose bib to the shutoff valve. The valve connects to the supply line with a sweated copper adapter.

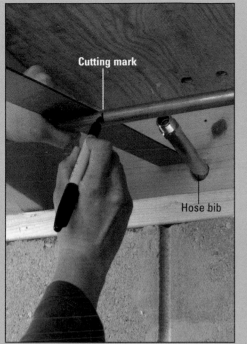

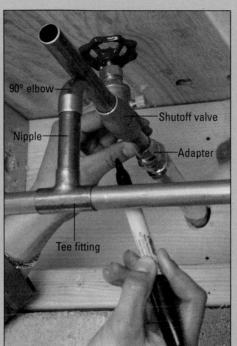

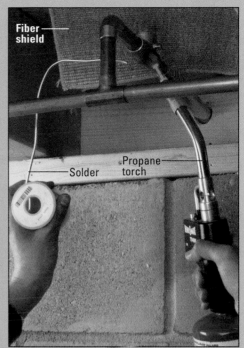

3 Hold a carpenter's square or straight board alongside the hose bib location and mark the cold-water pipe for the location of the tee fitting. **Shut off the water.** Cut into the pipe and install the fitting.

4 Dry-fit a nipple and an elbow to the tee. Dry-fit an adapter, a nipple, and a shutoff. (A dielectric fitting is not needed if the bib is chrome-plated brass.) Make sure the hose bib slopes so it drains when turned off. Place the final nipple in the valve and mark it for cutting.

5 Remove the inner parts of the shutoff valve. Protect the framing with a heat-proof fiber shield and sweat all the joints (see *pages 30–31*).

Galvanized-pipe connections

To break into a galvanized pipe, cut the supply pipe with a hack saw or reciprocating saw equipped with a metal-cutting blade (see *pages 36–37*), and remove pipe back to the nearest joint. Add sections of threaded pipe to reach the location of the hose bib.

Install a union and tee fitting and add a nipple and elbow to reach the level of the hose bib. (Build in a slight incline away from the hose bib.) Drill a finder hole and bore a 1⅛-inch hole (see Step 1, opposite). Add nipples and a union to reach a coupler attached to the hose bib.

If the supply line does not already have a stop valve in the near vicinity, add one between the union and the coupling.

CLEARING DRAIN LINES

When a sink, toilet, or tub becomes clogged, first try plunging. Bail out most of the water but leave a couple of inches so the plunger can seal tightly around the drain opening. Seal any openings—such as the overflow openings of a bathroom sink or a tub—by firmly pressing a wet rag into the opening. When plunging a double-bowl sink, seal the drain hole of the other bowl. If you have a dishwasher, clamp its drain hose tightly before plunging so you won't force water back into the dishwasher.

If plunging doesn't work, try hand augering, dismantling a trap, or forcing pressurized water into the drain. These techniques will almost certainly clear a clog for an individual drain.

If more than one drain is stopped or runs slowly, take more aggressive steps. Auger through an intermediate cleanout or trap. If that doesn't solve the problem, you may need to auger the main drain. Call on a plumbing company that specializes in clearing clogs or rent a power auger and do it yourself.

PRESTART CHECKLIST

☐ **TIME**
With a rented power auger, an hour or two to run it through a main drain

☐ **TOOLS**
Hand-crank or power auger, adjustable wrench, pipe wrench, groove-joint pliers, perhaps a hammer and chisel

☐ **SKILLS**
Identifying and opening traps and cleanouts

☐ **PREP**
Clear the area and prepare for cleaning up afterward.

☐ **MATERIALS**
Pipe-thread tape, replacement cleanout plug, bucket

Unclogging a house line

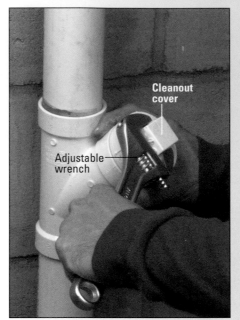

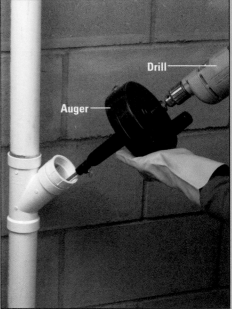

1 Remove a cleanout plug using an adjustable wrench or a pipe wrench. A cleanout usually provides access to the main or secondary stack.

2 An inexpensive auger like this one attaches to a standard drill. The resulting tool is more powerful and easier to use than a hand-crank auger (below).

TYPES OF TRAPS

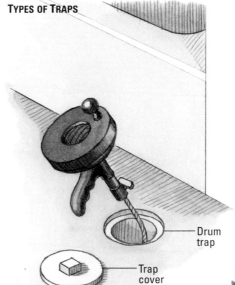

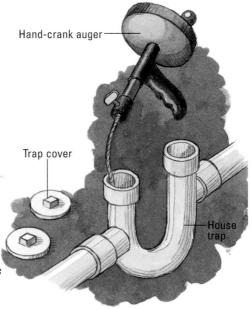

A single drain cover on a bathroom floor opens to a drum trap. A house trap typically has two trap covers near each other on the floor. Both can be augered.

Augering a main drain

Cleanout cover

Pipe wrench

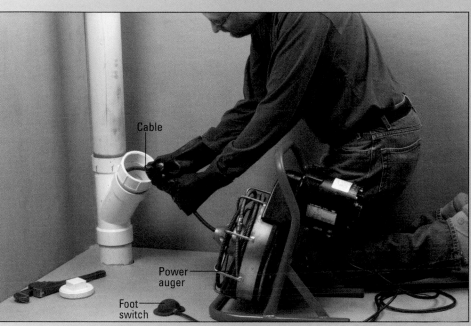

Cable

Power auger

Foot switch

1 The main drain—the line coming from the street to your house—may be clogged by tree roots that have grown into it. (Many old drain lines are made of clay or have permeable joints.) Open the cleanout plug. If you have a metal cleanout plug, you may have to loosen it with a hammer and chisel.

2 Rent a power auger with several bits to handle various problems. Rental staff can advise on which bit to use. Select the bit and attach it with the setscrew provided on the cable end. Position to auger close to the pipe to minimize the length of exposed cable. **Make sure machine or drop cords are not lying in water.** Plug in the auger. Wearing heavy rubber gloves, push the cable into the drain until you hit an obstruction. Switch on the auger and use the foot switch to start the cable rotating. Let it run for awhile, then turn off the auger and push the cable in farther.

Solving minor clogs

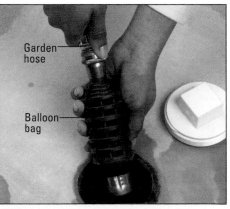

Garden hose

Balloon bag

Sink trap: If a kitchen or bathroom sink is chronically clogged, there may be debris in the trap. Place a bucket under the trap to collect spilled water. Loosen slip nuts with groove-joint pliers and disassemble the trap. Pull out any debris and reassemble. Replace all the slip washers that you disassemble.

Auger: If the clog is farther down the line, open a trap or drain line at a convenient point and auger the line. Using a hand-crank or drill-operated auger, insert the cable as far as it will go, tighten the setscrew, and start turning. When you feel the snake move forward, repeat. Augering will push a clog through or pull it out.

Balloon bag: Use pressurized water to push a clog through. Attach a balloon bag (make sure it's the right size for your pipe) to a garden hose and push the bag into the pipe until it hits the clog. Turn on the water. The balloon fills with water (sealing off the pipe) while releasing a stream of water to break up the clog.

REPLACING A VALVE

A plumbing system should have a main shutoff valve that controls water to the whole house and intermediate shutoff valves that control water for various areas of the house. There also should be shutoff valves on the incoming cold supply line for a water heater and stop valves (also called fixture shutoffs) that control water leading to individual faucets and appliances.

If an old shutoff valve—usually a gate or globe type—leaks at the packing nut, make sure it's all the way open or closed. If it still leaks, try tightening the packing nut with pliers or a adjustable wrench. (Don't crank down too hard, or you could crack the nut.) If it still leaks, or if it fails to completely shut water off, follow the steps at right to repair or replace it.

Stop valves are often cheaply made and may fail to shut water off completely or may leak from the packing nut. Replace a faulty stop valve with a ball-type model, which costs a little more but is very reliable.

A globe valve inhibits water flow even if it is in good working order. Replacing it with a ball valve may increase water pressure.

PRESTART CHECKLIST

☐ **TIME**
An hour or two to repair or replace a shutoff valve

☐ **TOOLS**
Groove-joint pliers, pipe wrenches, screwdriver, torch, wire brush

☐ **SKILLS**
Working with supply pipe

☐ **PREP**
Shut off water upstream from the valve.

☐ **MATERIALS**
Repair parts or a new valve, pipe-thread tape, flux and solder

Servicing an old valve

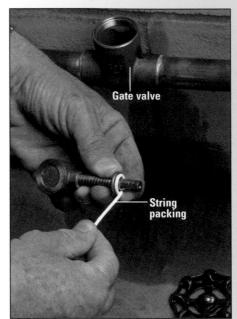

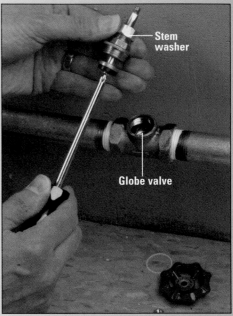

If water leaks from the packing nut of a gate valve, replace the packing washer or the string packing. If the valve does not shut water off completely, try removing the gate and cleaning out any debris in the valve body. If that does not solve the problem, replace the valve.

If water leaks out the packing nut of a globe valve, replace the packing washer or string packing. If the valve fails to shut off water completely, replace the stem washer with an exact replacement. If that does not solve the problem, replace the valve.

GLOBE, GATE, AND BALL VALVES

A globe valve has a stem washer that presses against the chamber to shut off water. A gate valve has a wedge-shaped gate (shown) that moves up and down, or a cylindrical gate that pivots, to control water flow. A ball valve has a spherical gate that opens or closes when the handle rotates a quarter turn.

Globe valve   Gate valve   Ball valve

Installing a new valve

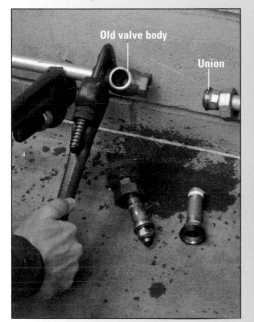

1 If possible, open a nearby union and disassemble a few pipes to get to the existing valve. If not, follow the steps on *pages 36–37* for breaking into steel pipe. If the supply pipes are copper, see *pages 30–31*.

2 The new valve will be about the same size as the old one, so you shouldn't have to change any pipe lengths. (Otherwise have on hand a selection of nipples.) Wrap all threaded pipe ends with several windings of pipe-thread tape and assemble the parts.

3 Tighten the pipes and fittings as you go using two 14-inch pipe wrenches. Finish by assembling and tightening a union. Test for leaks.

Installing stop valves

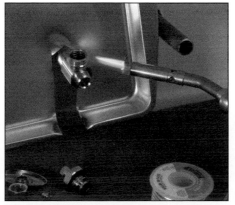

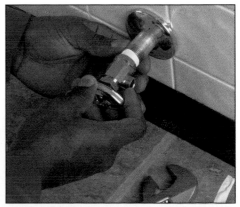

Purchase a stop valve that fits your size and type of pipe. A compression-type valve is the easiest to install on copper pipe. Slip the nut, ferrule, and valve on the pipe. Slide the ferrule and nut over and tighten the nut.

You can choose a valve that sweats onto a copper pipe. Remove the inner parts of the valve and protect nearby areas against damage from the flame. Brush or sand the inside of the valve and the outside of the pipe. Apply flux, assemble, heat the valve with a torch, apply solder, and wipe the joint *(pages 30–31).*

A threaded stop valve is the easiest to install. Wrap the pipe end with several windings of pipe-thread tape, screw on the valve, and tighten with an adjustable wrench.

INSTALLING A NEW BATHROOM

Installing a new bathroom with a toilet, sink, and tub may well be the most challenging do-it-yourself project you'll ever tackle. You'll need a thorough understanding of plumbing systems and techniques, a good helper, and the patience to keep at it until you get everything right.

Getting a handle on the plumbing

The following pages show how to install the three major bathroom plumbing fixtures in a common configuration. You'll find quite a few variations on this basic arrangement. Your situation may call for pipe runs that differ from those shown, so you may need to develop a unique plan that suits your home.

You'll need a good understanding of the basic skills and techniques of plumbing. Study the first chapter of this book, then develop a general plan for hooking the new plumbing to the old. Pay special attention to the drain vents and make sure you use pipe types and sizes that conform to code. If possible, hire a professional plumber to spend an hour or two giving you advice. This modest investment could save time and money later on.

The entire project

Whether you are remodeling an existing bathroom or installing one in a new addition, you will need carpentry skills. Modifying the framing sometimes can make the plumbing work easier. Plan and install the plumbing so it damages joists and studs as little as possible; reinforce any framing members that have been compromised. It's usually best to run any electrical lines after the plumbing has been installed.

A complete bath installation calls for thorough planning, advanced plumbing skills, and patience.

CHAPTER PREVIEW

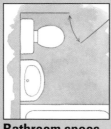

Bathroom specs
page 80

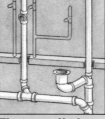

The overall plan
page 81

Preparing the site
page 82

Running drain and vent lines
page 84

Capping off supply lines allows you to test your work before installing final fittings; cap the lines, turn on the water, and check for leaks. Caps also keep out debris that could later clog faucets and spouts.

Tape off all drain openings or buy ready-made caps or fittings with knockouts.

Running copper supply lines
page 90

Hooking up the tub or shower faucet
page 92

Installing a whirlpool tub
page 94

Connecting the toilet and sink
page 98

Roughing in supply, drain, and vent lines is the most demanding part of a plumbing project. Once an inspector has approved the essentials of your project, you can finish the walls and install fixtures, hardware, and trim. In the meantime, seal all drain openings to keep debris from falling into drain lines and sewer gas from entering the house.

BATHROOM SPECS

Specifications for the placement of plumbing fixtures and the dimensions of pipes are intended to make the bathroom a comfortable room with plenty of capacity for incoming water and outgoing drains and vents. The specs shown here will meet the requirements of most building departments, but check local codes to be sure.

Bathroom layout
Where you place the toilet, sink, and tub may depend partly on the existing plumbing. Most homes have a "wet wall," an interior wall that is thicker than most walls because it contains the main stack. Minimize long horizontal runs of drain and vent pipes by installing fixtures close to the wet wall.

Also plan for a layout that is comfortable and convenient. The following pages show how to install a basic 5×8-foot bathroom—just enough room for the three major fixtures with adequate space between them.

Most codes require that no fixture be closer than 15 inches from a toilet's centerline. There must be at least 24 inches of space in front of the toilet (it's OK for a door to swing into this space).

Sinks and vanity sink tops range from 20 to 30 inches in width. A standard bathtub is 60 inches by 32 inches. If your plans call for a larger tub, alter the layout to fit it. The tub shown on *pages 94–97* will be 36 inches wide once framing and tiles are installed.

The framing—not the finished wall—must be 60 inches wide to accommodate a standard tub length. If the opening is any smaller, the tub will not fit; if the opening is more than ¼ inch too long, making a tight seal along the wall will be difficult. Framing must be almost perfectly square.

Choosing materials
These plans call for 3-inch PVC pipe for the main drain and the short length leading from the toilet to the drain, and 2-inch PVC for the other drain lines and the vents. Local codes may call for a 4-inch main drain, and some plumbers prefer to run larger vent pipes.

Cast-iron drainpipe is making a comeback in some areas because it's quieter than plastic pipe. However, cast-iron should be installed by a pro. (You can reduce the noise of water draining through PVC by wrapping the pipe with insulation.)

Rigid copper pipe is the most common material for supply lines. However, PEX or other plastic materials may be permitted in your area. Bathrooms are usually supplied with ½-inch pipe. For maximum water pressure, however, run ¾-inch pipe to the bathroom and use ½-inch for short runs only.

MINIMUM CLEARANCES

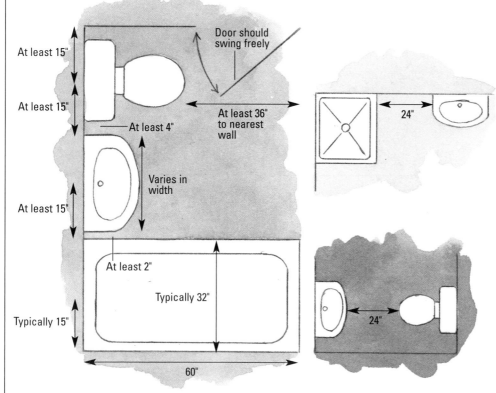

A bathroom with a 5×8-foot interior space allows the minimum clearances that most municipal codes require for fixtures. While exploring layout options, maintain these clearances in your plan to assure ease of use and installation.

Standard dimensions

Make sure your plans follow these standard specs:

Drain and vent pipes
Toilet: 3–4 inches; 2-inch vent
Sink: 2-inch drain, connecting to 3-inch horizontal run; 2-inch vent
Tub/shower: 2 inch, connecting to 3-inch horizontal run; 2-inch vent
Main stack: 3–4 inches
Sink drain: 19 inches above floor
Toilet drain: 12 inches from wall

Supply pipes
Tub/shower: ¾-inch pipe
Sink, toilet: ½-inch pipe
Sink stubout: 19 inches above floor, 8–10 inches apart
Toilet stubout: 8 inches above floor

Tub/shower fittings
Tub control(s): 28 inches from floor
Spout: 6 inches above top edge
Shower head arm: About 76 inches above floor
Shower control: 48 inches above floor

THE OVERALL PLAN

Once you have decided on the basic layout and have a general idea of how the drain and vents will run, make specific plans. Measure the existing room and/or plan for new framing right down to the inch; take into account the thickness of the wall finishing material—usually ½ inch for drywall and perhaps another ⅜ inch for wall tiles. (See *pages 26–27* for tips on producing drawings.)

Vents

Start by figuring the vents; see *pages 10–11.* As a general rule, the drain line for each fixture should connect to a vent within a few feet of the fixture. A true vent never has water running through it, although "wet venting" is permitted under some circumstances.

This plan calls for running a new vent up through the ceiling and either tying into an existing vent in the attic or running out through the roof. Or you may be able to tie into an existing vent on the same floor.

Consider how new lines will affect existing vents. For instance, if you install an upper-story bathroom and tie into an existing stack, you may end up draining water through a pipe that is now used as a vent.

Drains

In this plan, a new main drain line for the bathroom runs down to the floor below. If the new bathroom is on the first floor, you can probably simply tie into the house's main drain line in the basement or crawlspace below. If the new bathroom is on the second floor, the bathroom's main drain will have to travel through the wall on the first floor and down to the basement or crawlspace. (See *page 83* for how to trace the location of a drainpipe through an intervening story.)

If a drain line is nearby, you may choose to run a new drainpipe across the floor to join to it, rather than running a new line. However, it may be difficult to run a toilet's 3-inch (or 4-inch) drain through a floor, especially if you have to go through joists.

In the room below, the drain lines turn outward at a 45-degree angle to avoid running 3–4 inch pipe through studs. If the room below is finished, you will need to build a soffit around these pipes *(page 82)*. Or you can run the pipes through the studs. This plan calls for a 3-inch horizontal drain; codes may permit 2-inch pipe instead.

Seal openings where pipes enter attics or crawlspaces to prevent drafts and to act as fire stops.

BATHROOM SUPPLY, DRAIN-WASTE-VENT OVERVIEW

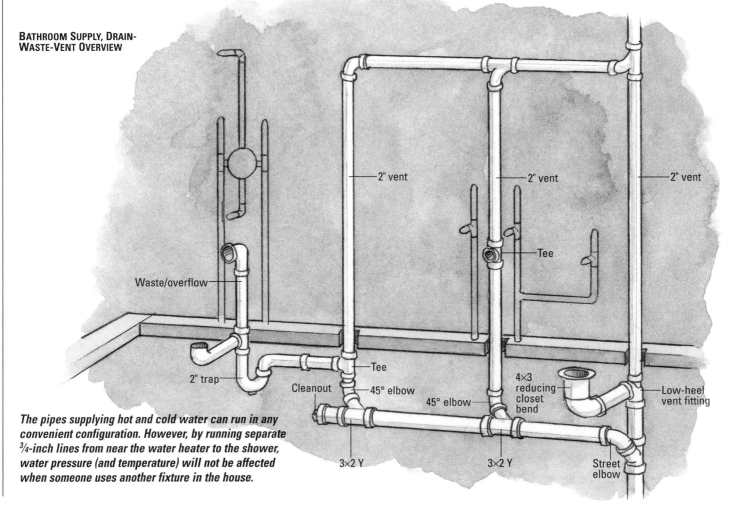

The pipes supplying hot and cold water can run in any convenient configuration. However, by running separate ¾-inch lines from near the water heater to the shower, water pressure (and temperature) will not be affected when someone uses another fixture in the house.

PREPARING THE SITE

An installation like this typically requires an extra-wide "wet wall" built of 2×6s or two side-by-side 2×4 walls. However, since only 2-inch pipe runs through the walls, codes sometimes permit a standard 2×4 wall. Unless you live in an area with a warm climate, avoid running pipes in an exterior wall.

To carve a new bathroom out of existing rooms, you may need to move a wall. (For more information on moving or building walls, see *Stanley Interior Walls.*) Before removing a wall, make sure it's not load-bearing; check with a carpenter or structural engineer if you are not sure.

Whether you are framing a new space or remodeling an existing space, make sure the framing accommodates the tub.

Remove drywall or plaster from the areas where you will run plumbing. Clear out all cabinets, fixtures, and other obstructions.

If wiring is in the path of plumbing, shut off power to the circuit and test to make sure. You may want to remove cables and reinstall them after the plumbing is in place.

PRESTART CHECKLIST

☐ **TIME**
A day or more to remove wall coverings; about half a day to mark for positions of fixtures

☐ **TOOLS**
Hammer, pry bar, level, framing square, drill, hole saw, saber saw, circular saw, reciprocating saw

☐ **SKILLS**
Basic carpentry skills, planning for plumbing runs, careful measuring

☐ **PREP**
Have your plumbing plans approved by your building department.

☐ **MATERIALS**
Lumber for any framing that's needed

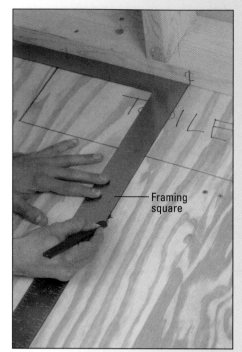

Framing square

1 Determine the exact center of the toilet drain. For most toilets, this is 12 inches from the finished wall surface. If you will install ½-inch drywall, measure 12½ inches out from the framing. (Toilets with drains set 10- and 14-inch from the wall are available, though usually in white only.)

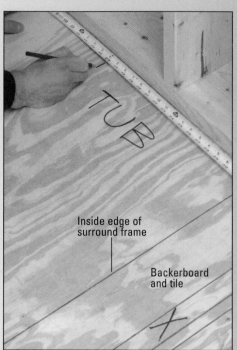

Inside edge of surround frame

Backerboard and tile

2 Study the instructions that come with the tub and the waste-and-overflow assembly to determine exactly where the tub drain needs to be *(pages 46–51)*. Mark the tub outline on the floor. In this case, the framing, backer board, and tiling for a whirlpool tub must be added.

PLANNING FOR FINISHING THE ROOM BELOW

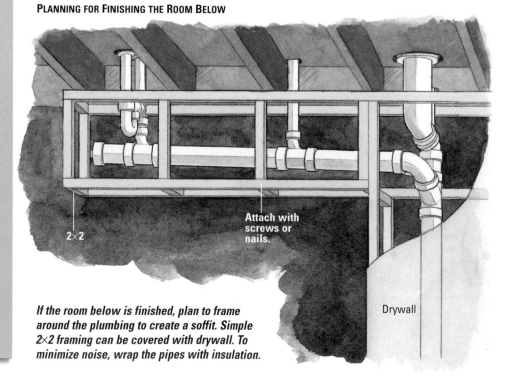

2×2

Attach with screws or nails.

Drywall

If the room below is finished, plan to frame around the plumbing to create a soffit. Simple 2×2 framing can be covered with drywall. To minimize noise, wrap the pipes with insulation.

Tub supply location

Sink drain, marked for cutting with hole saw

Notch marked for drain/vent fitting

Circular saw

Hole for toilet drain

Reciprocating saw

3 Mark the bottom plate for the location of the vent and drainpipes. Position the tub/shower vent so it will not interfere with the installation of the faucet *(pages 92–93)*. You may need to move a stud or two to make room for the tub/shower faucet. Also mark where the supply lines will enter the room. Check all your measurements twice.

4 Use a hole saw or saber saw to cut a hole in the floor for the toilet drain. Use a circular saw and a reciprocating saw to cut a section of flooring large enough to allow you to run the plumbing. Wherever you need to run pipes through joists, give yourself plenty of room to work.

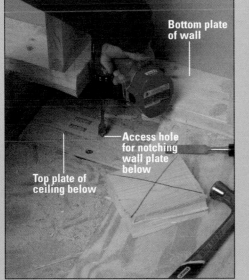

Bottom plate of wall

Access hole for notching wall plate below

Top plate of ceiling below

Hole cutting saw

5 Drill holes or cut notches as needed. To make room for the toilet drain *(page 84)*, a large notch must be cut in the bottom plate of the wall and the top plate of the ceiling below.

6 Using a hole saw, cut 2¼-inch holes for the tub and sink drains. Remove a 12×14-inch section of flooring for the tub/shower drain—cut a larger opening if you don't have access from behind or below.

STANLEY PRO TIP:

Running pipe through an intervening story

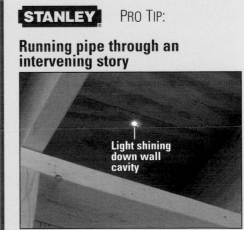

Light shining down wall cavity

If the new bathroom is on the second story, you will need to run a drainpipe down the wall of a first-story room. Don't tear into the wall to confirm the drain location. Instead, cut the bathroom drain hole and position a bright light over it. Take measurements and drill a test hole in the basement. If the location is right, you'll see the light.

RUNNING DRAIN AND VENT LINES

Because they are complicated and in some cases must be positioned precisely, drain and vent lines should be installed before the supply pipes. However, sometimes it may be possible to simplify supply runs by moving a vent pipe over a few inches.

If you must run drainpipes across a floor, carefully calculate the altitude—the amount of vertical room available—so you can pitch the drainpipe at ⅛ to ¼ inch per running foot.

Sometimes it's difficult to visualize just how drainpipes will travel through walls and floors. Once you start assembling the pieces and testing them for fit, you may need to modify your plans.

Some inspectors want horizontal vent pipes to be sloped so moisture caused by condensation can run back to the drainpipes; others don't consider this important. Err on the safe side and slope the vents.

PRESTART CHECKLIST

☐ **TIME**
Working with a helper, about two days to install drain and vent lines for a simple bathroom

☐ **TOOLS**
PVC saw or power saw, level, reciprocating saw, drill, carpentry tools

☐ **SKILLS**
Cutting and joining PVC pipe, running pipes through walls, connecting new pipe to old

☐ **PREP**
Have your plans approved by an inspector; prepare the room (pages 82–83).

☐ **MATERIALS**
PVC pipe and fittings to meet codes, fitting to join to existing drainpipe, PVC primer and cement, pipe strap

A. Running the main drain line

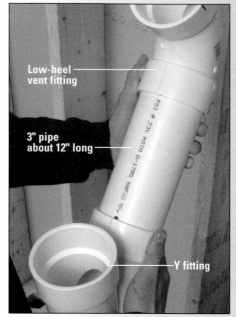

Low-heel vent fitting

3" pipe about 12" long

Y fitting

Low-heel vent fitting

Y fitting

1 Start with a length of 3-inch pipe long enough to reach the basement or crawlspace (Step 5, *page 86*). You may be able to cut it to exact length after it has been installed. Dry-fit a Y fitting, a length of pipe, and a low-heel vent fitting as shown, lining them up precisely.

2 Insert the assembly down through the wall plates and temporarily anchor it. Make sure the Y fitting is low enough to allow for installation of the other drain lines (Step 2, *page 87*). Once you are sure of the configuration, pull up the assembly and prime and glue the pieces.

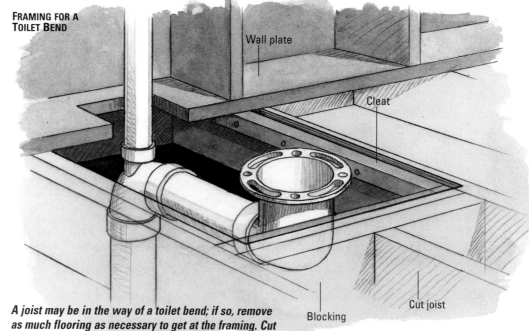

FRAMING FOR A TOILET BEND

Wall plate

Cleat

Blocking

Cut joist

A joist may be in the way of a toilet bend; if so, remove as much flooring as necessary to get at the framing. Cut the joist, install a blocking piece, and attach 2×4 cleats around the opening.

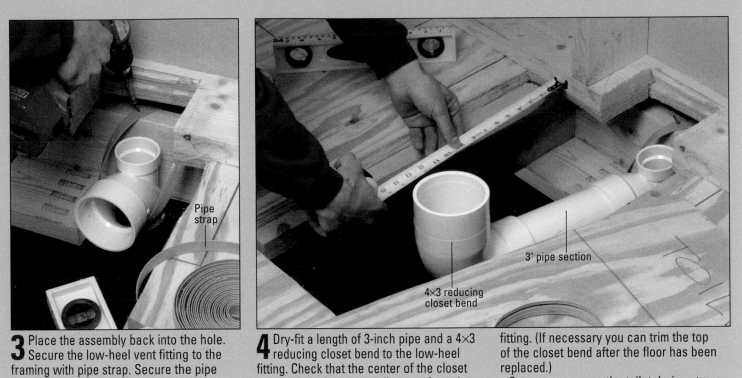

Pipe strap

4×3 reducing closet bend

3" pipe section

3 Place the assembly back into the hole. Secure the low-heel vent fitting to the framing with pipe strap. Secure the pipe from below as well.

4 Dry-fit a length of 3-inch pipe and a 4×3 reducing closet bend to the low-heel fitting. Check that the center of the closet bend hole is the correct distance from the wall — in most cases 12½ inches from the framing to allow for ½-inch drywall. Check that the pipe slopes ⅛ to ¼ inch down to the fitting. (If necessary you can trim the top of the closet bend after the floor has been replaced.)

Once you are sure the toilet drain setup is correct, mark the alignment of the fittings and disassemble. Glue the pieces together. Support the closet bend with a strap.

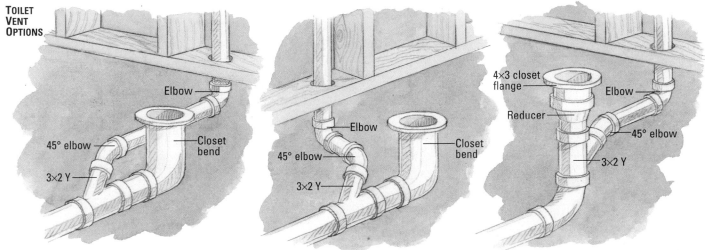

TOILET VENT OPTIONS

Elbow
45° elbow
Closet bend
3×2 Y

Elbow
45° elbow
Closet bend
3×2 Y

4×3 closet flange
Elbow
Reducer
45° elbow
3×2 Y

If the toilet drain does not connect directly to a vent, you must find another way to vent it. If the drain line runs away from the wall where you want the vent, use a reducing Y and a 45-degree street elbow to point the vent line toward the wall. The horizontal vent pipe runs right next to the closet bend.

If the vent wall is parallel to the drain pipe, install a 45-degree reducing Y and a street elbow to point toward the wall. You may need another elbow (of any degree) to position the vertical vent where you want it.

If the vent wall is opposite the drain line, use a reducing Y and a street elbow. The fittings can be pointed straight at the wall or at an angle, as needed.

Running the main drain line (continued)

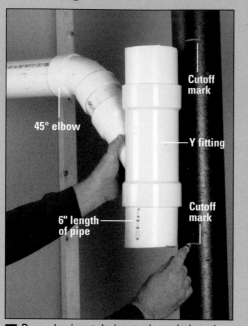

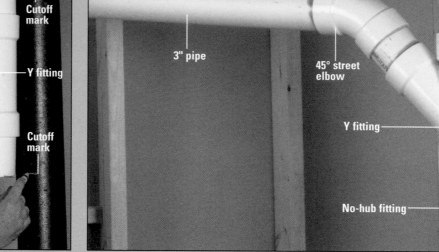

5 Run a horizontal pipe to the existing pipe and assemble the parts needed for tying into it. All fittings should be Ys or drain elbows so wastewater can flow easily. Hold the horizontal pipe so it's sloped at ⅛ to ¼ inch per foot and mark the existing pipe for cutting *(pages 42–43).*

6 If the existing pipe is cast-iron, take care to support it securely before cutting. In the setup shown, a 4×3 Y connects to the house drain using no-hub fittings (which should be used to connect to either cast iron or ABS). Once you are sure the fittings are correct and the horizontal pipe slopes correctly, make alignment marks. Disassemble the parts, apply primer, and reassemble the pieces in order, starting at the existing drain.

OTHER DRAIN CONFIGURATIONS

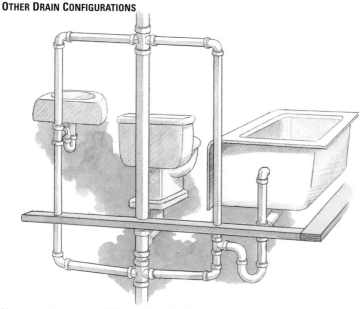

Your situation may call for another drain configuration. This example shows a single-floor home in which all the fixtures tie into horizontal pipes, which in turn run to the stack.

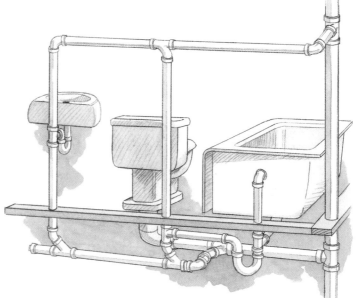

In this example for a two-story home, first-floor vent pipes run up to join the second-floor vents at the top of their runs, so that all the vents tie in at a point well above the second-floor fixtures.

B. Running individual drain lines

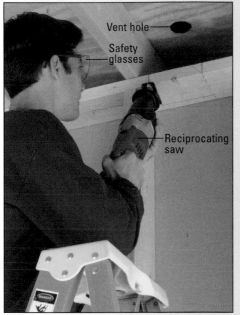

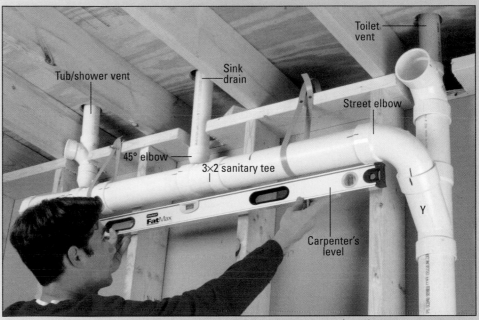

1 Slip lengths of 2-inch pipe down through the holes drilled in the floor plate for the tub and sink vents. Have a helper hold the pipes plumb as you mark the plate below for notching. Cut notches about an inch wider than the pipe to accommodate a fitting.

2 Cut and dry-fit the horizontal drainpipe and the fittings for connecting the tub and the sink drains. (A 3-inch horizontal pipe is shown, but your inspector may permit a 2-inch pipe.) Insert a street elbow into the Y and hold the other pieces in place to mark for cutting. Make sure the horizontal pipe slopes at a rate of ⅛ to ¼ inch per running foot. Install a reducing tee and a 45-degree elbow (or street elbow if you need to save room) for both joints. If the pipe will be accessible, install a cleanout on the fitting for the tub; otherwise, install a drain elbow instead of a tee.

WHAT IF...
You need to run a drain for a shower only?

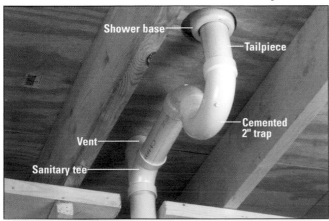

A 1½-inch drain trap is often permitted for a shower, but a 2-inch trap will ensure quick flow of water and will be less likely to clog. A shower has no waste-and-overflow assembly, so the rough plumbing consists of a cemented trap that rises to the correct height for the shower base *(page 54)*.

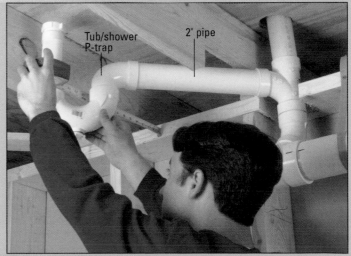

3 To plumb the drain for the tub, dry-fit a 2-inch trap onto a length of 2-inch pipe that is longer than it needs to be. Study the directions for the tub to determine precisely where the trap should be located. Hold the trap-and-pipe assembly in place and mark it for a cut. Dry fit and check that the horizontal pipe slopes correctly. Once all the parts are accurately assembled, draw alignment marks and prime and glue the pieces together.

C. Install the vents

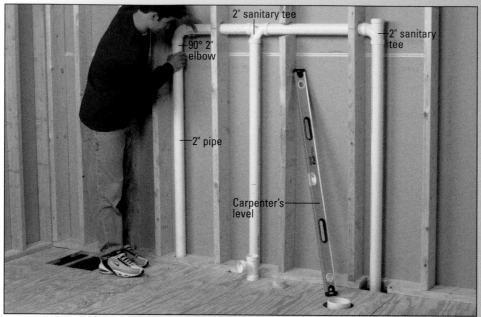

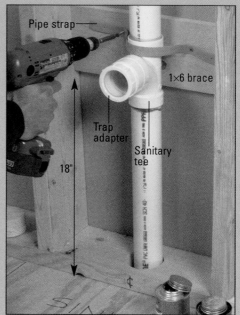

1 Your codes may require the horizontal revent lines be as high as 54 inches above the finished floor, or at least 6 inches above the fixture flood level (the point where water will start to spill out). Use a carpenter's level to mark the studs for drilling holes. Run the horizontal vent lines sloped downward toward the fixtures at a rate of 1/8 to 1/4 inch per running foot. Drill holes, cut pipes, and connect them in a dry run using drain fittings.

2 Install a sanitary tee facing into the room for the sink trap. The ideal height is usually 18 inches above the finished floor, but check your sink instructions to be sure. Cement a 1 1/4-inch trap adapter into the tee. Install a piece of 1×6 blocking and anchor the pipe with a strap.

RUNNING A VENT AROUND AN OBSTRUCTION

If a medicine cabinet, window, or other obstruction prevents you from running a vent straight up, you'll have to turn a corner for a short distance, then turn again to head upwards. Horizontal runs should be at least 6 inches above the fixture flood level—the rim of a sink, for example .

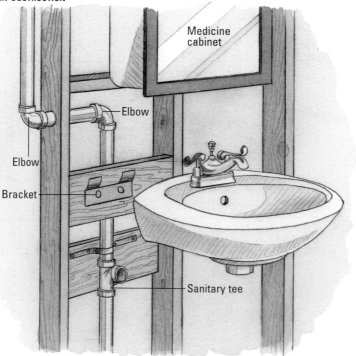

Running up through the ceiling

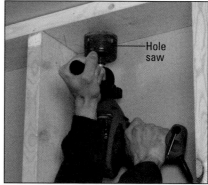

To run a vent pipe through the ceiling, first drill a test hole to make sure you won't bump into any joists in the attic. You may need to move the hole over a few inches. The top plate may be doubled, meaning you have to drill through 3 inches. You may need to drill with a hole saw first from below (shown), then from above.

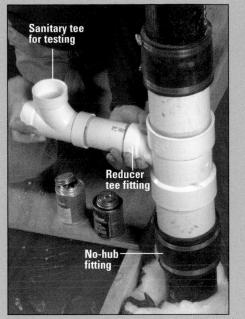

Sanitary tee
for testing

Reducer
tee fitting

No-hub
fitting

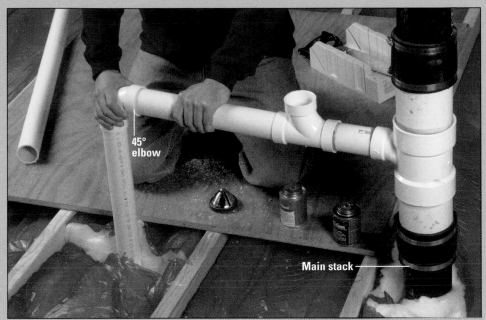

45°
elbow

Main stack

3 In the attic, tap into a conveniently located vent pipe. Following the steps shown on *pages 42–43*, cut the pipe and connect a reducer tee fitting. Use no-hub fittings to connect a PVC fitting to cast-iron or ABS pipe.

4 Run the new vent line over to the tee fitting. The pipes should slope gently down away from the existing vent pipe so water can travel downward.

Your inspector may want you to include a tee fitting to be used for testing: Once the

drain system is assembled and cemented, plug the drain pipe at the lower end. Pour water into it until all the drain and vent pipes are filled with water. Allow the water to sit for a day to make sure there are no leaks.

INSTALLING A ROOF JACK

Check local codes for the correct way to install a roof jack. In most areas you will need to install a 4-inch pipe. Some areas allow for a plastic pipe to extend out the roof (shown); in other areas a metal pipe is required. Purchase a roof jack with a rubber flange that will seal a 4-inch pipe.

Cut the 4-inch pipe to roughly the same angle as the roof slope and hold it plumb, its top touching the attic ceiling. Mark for the hole, which will be oval. Cut the hole using a drill and a reciprocating saw.

You may need to cut some roofing shingles back. Slip the jack under the roof shingles at its upper half; the lower half of the jack rests on top of shingles. Poke the vent pipe up through the rubber flange. To anchor the jack, lift up some shingles and drive roofing nails. If any nails are not covered by shingles, cover the heads with roofing cement.

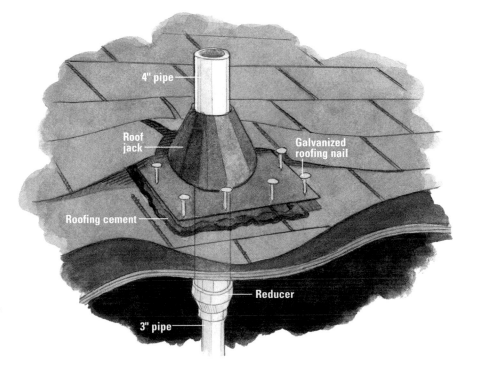

4" pipe

Roof
jack

Galvanized
roofing nail

Roofing cement

Reducer

3" pipe

RUNNING COPPER SUPPLY LINES

Rigid copper is the material of choice for supply lines in most locales, although flexible or rigid plastic is permitted in some areas. An hour or two of practice will prepare you to cut copper pipe and sweat joints quickly and securely *(pages 30–31)*.

Supply lines can be routed along almost any path, although extending a pipe run and adding bends will lower water pressure slightly. This plan shows running pipes so that they do not cross drainpipes or vents. In most cases, it's easier to make the horizontal runs below the room in the crawlspace or basement. If you need to run pipes horizontally in the room, see the box on *page 91*.

Installing hammer arresters (Step 3) ensures against a banging noise when you turn on or off a faucet.

Copper pipe can last for many decades. However, it is easily punctured or dented. Position it out of harm's way and install nailing plates to the studs to protect pipes against errant nails.

Hot water is always on the left, cold water on the right.

PRESTART CHECKLIST

☐ **TIME**
About half a day to run supply lines for a sink and toilet

☐ **TOOLS**
Drill, bit and bit extender, propane torch, tubing cutter, multiuse wire brush, flame guard, groove-joint pliers, carpentry tools for installing braces

☐ **SKILLS**
Accurate measuring and drilling, working with copper pipe

☐ **PREP**
Install all or most of the drain and vent pipes; determine the supply routes.

☐ **MATERIALS**
Copper pipe and fittings, flux, solder, damp rag

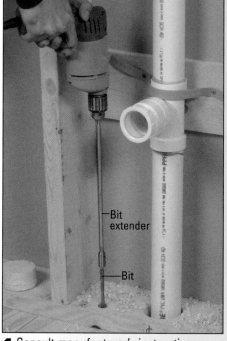

1 Consult manufacturer's instructions to position pipes for the shower faucet, sink, and toilet. For example, the shower faucet in this plan calls for vertical pipes 10 inches apart. Use a spade bit attached to a bit extender to drill holes in the center of the wall plate, if possible.

2 Install cross braces so you can anchor the pipes firmly. Cut pieces of 2×4 or 1×4 to fit snugly between studs and attach them by drilling pilot holes and driving screws. If you plan to install a pedestal sink *(page 99)*, attach a 2×6 or a ¾-inch plywood brace (shown) to support its bracket.

Running and securing supply pipes

A copper supply strap attaches to the face of the studs. Pipes fit into notches or holes, sized and spaced for correct placement. The pipes can be soldered onto the strap using the same techniques as for sweating fittings.

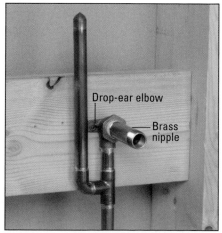

A drop-ear elbow makes the most secure attachment. If you use one, the hammer arrester must be connected to a tee and an elbow just below the drop-ear elbow. Insert a brass threaded nipple into the elbow.

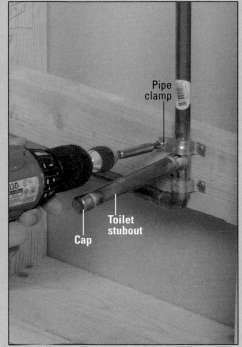

3 Tie into existing supply lines *(page 43)*. The hot and cold stubouts usually should be 8–10 inches apart and 19 to 23 inches above the floor; consult the manufacturer's instructions to be sure. A toilet stubout is usually 8 inches above the floor.

Dry-fit a complete assemble for the sink and the toilet. For each stubout, use a tee fitting, a 6-inch length of pipe (which you will cut off later), and a cap to protect the pipe. Install a hammer arrester to each.

4 Sweat all the parts following instructions on *pages 30–31*. Anchor the pipes with at least one—preferably two—clamps at each stubout.

STANLEY PRO TIP

Tap into shower supplies

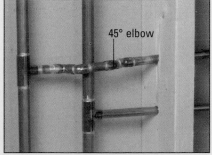

Rather than running sink supply lines from below, you may want to run them horizontally from the shower. If the shower lines are ¾ inch, use reducer tees to tap into the lines. Use 45-degree elbows to snake one line past the other (in this case, the hot past the vertical cold-water line). If the sink is used at the same time as the shower, water temperature will change.

WHAT IF...
Supply lines must run past drain or vent pipes?

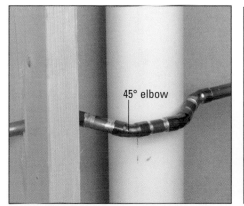

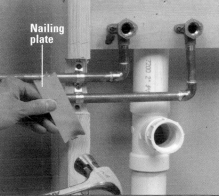

To run supplies around an obstruction such as a drain or vent pipe, use four 45-degree elbows. This arrangement makes for smoother water flow and less loss of water pressure than using 90-degree elbows.

Another option is to cut notches rather than holes and run supply pipes in front of the vent pipes. If you do this, be sure to install protective nailing plates or the pipes could be punctured by a nail when the drywall is installed.

HOOKING UP A SHOWER OR TUB FAUCET

This plan calls for separate ¾-inch lines to supply the shower. This ensures good water pressure and protects anyone in the shower from a sudden change of temperature when a faucet is turned on or the toilet tank refills. Tap into the house's cold and hot water lines as near to the water heater as possible.

Choose the tub or shower faucet before you start installing pipes. Read the manufacturer's directions carefully so you know exactly where the pipes should go.

If your faucet does not have integrated shutoff valves (see box, *opposite*), install reachable shutoff valves on the lines leading to the shower so you can easily turn off the water if repairs are needed.

Assuming an 18-inch-tall tub, position the faucet about 28 inches above the floor for a tub, about 48 inches for a shower. You may want to compromise and position it about 38 inches above the floor.

PRESTART CHECKLIST

☐ **TIME**
About half a day to run supply lines and install a tub/shower faucet

☐ **TOOLS**
Drill, propane torch, tubing cutter, multi-use wire brush, flame guard, damp rag, groove-joint pliers

☐ **SKILLS**
Accurate measuring and drilling, working with copper pipe

☐ **PREP**
Tap into the hot and cold water lines and run ¾-inch pipe up into the room. If needed, move a stud to make room for the plumbing behind the tub.

☐ **MATERIALS**
Tub/shower faucet, copper pipe and fittings, flux, solder, pipe-thread tape

Cross brace

1× scrap stands for ½" backer board plus ¼" tile.

1 Most faucets come with a plastic cover that protects the faucet and serves as a guide for the depth at which it must be set. To determine where to place the braces, consider the total thickness of the finished wall—often ½-inch-thick backer board plus ¼-inch-thick tiles.

2×6 cross brace

2 Determine how high you want the spout (make sure it will clear the tub), the faucet handles, and the showerhead. Install a 2×6 brace for each. Anchor the braces with screws rather than nails so you can move them more easily if they need adjustment.

TUB/SHOWER INSTALLATION

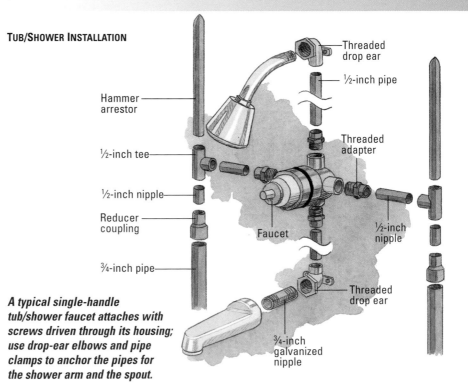

Threaded drop ear
½-inch pipe
Hammer arrestor
Threaded adapter
½-inch tee
½-inch nipple
Reducer coupling
Faucet
½-inch nipple
¾-inch pipe
Threaded drop ear
¾-inch galvanized nipple

A typical single-handle tub/shower faucet attaches with screws driven through its housing; use drop-ear elbows and pipe clamps to anchor the pipes for the shower arm and the spout.

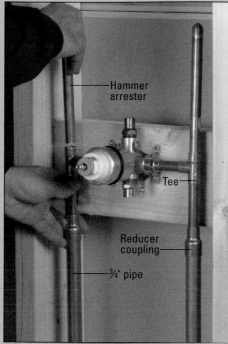

Hammer arrester

Tee

Reducer coupling

¾" pipe

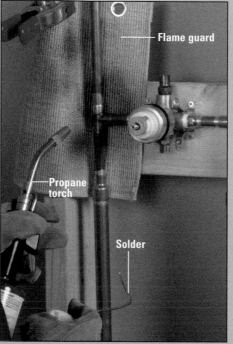

Flame guard

Propane torch

Solder

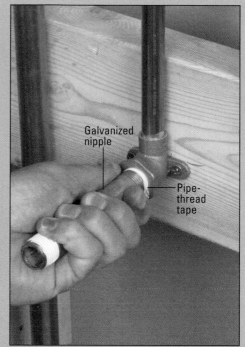

Galvanized nipple

Pipe-thread tape

3 Assemble all the pipes in a dry run. Install ¾-inch pipe up to the height of the shower, add reducing couplings or elbows, and run short lengths of ½-inch pipe to the threaded adapters on the faucet. Anchor the faucet according to manufacturer's directions.

4 Once you are sure of the connections, sweat all the fittings *(pages 30–31)*. Start at the faucet, then move on to the shower arm and spout connections. Run ½-inch pipe up to the shower arm and down to the spout; attach drop-ear elbows at both spots.

5 Finger-tighten a threaded nipple—either brass or galvanized—into both drop-ear elbows. Once the wall covering is in place, remove them and install the shower arm and the tub spout.

**STANLEY** PRO TIP

Add reinforcement to shower-arm dropears

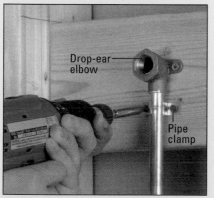

Drop-ear elbow

Pipe clamp

Whacking the showerhead with your elbow can bend or crack a drop ear elbow. As an extra safeguard, screw a pipe clamp just below the drop-ear.

WHAT IF...
You have other faucet setups?

Three-handle faucet setup

Integral shutoff

Adapter

A three-handle faucet may require that supply pipes be spread farther apart than for a single-handle faucet. Threaded adapters screw in for the supplies, spout, or shower arm.

A faucet with integral shutoffs comes with a large escutcheon (coverplate), so you can more easily reach the shutoff valves.

INSTALLING A WHIRLPOOL TUB

Some whirlpool tubs (also called spas) have a finished side or two, so framing for the side panel and tiling are not required. Rectangular models install much like a standard tub *(pages 49–51)*, except that a GFCI electrical receptacle is required. Triangular whirlpools fit into a corner.

The drop-in model shown on these pages fits into a frame. No special supply lines are needed; the whirlpool circulates water after it's filled by a standard spout. Some models have heaters to keep the water hot without replenishing. Other models have their own spouts; follow manufacturer's instructions for running supply lines.

Large whirlpools are very heavy when filled with water, so you may need to strengthen the floor by adding joists. Check the whirlpool's instructions and local codes.

Ideally it's best to lay flooring after the tub is framed and installed but before tiling.

PRESTART CHECKLIST

☐ **TIME**
Two or three days to frame, install, and tile a whirlpool tub

☐ **TOOLS**
Carpentry tools, groove-joint pliers, PVC saw, wiring tools, tiling tools, putty knife, screwdriver, adjustable wrench

☐ **SKILLS**
Connecting PVC pipe, basic carpentry, basic wiring, installing tiles

☐ **PREP**
Measure the space carefully, taking into account the framing, backerboard, and tile thickness.

☐ **MATERIALS**
Whirlpool tub, waste-and-overflow unit, lumber and screws for framing, GFCI receptacle, cable, breaker, cement backerboard with screws, mortar mix, tile, mastic, grout, caulk, spacers, pipe thread tape, rag

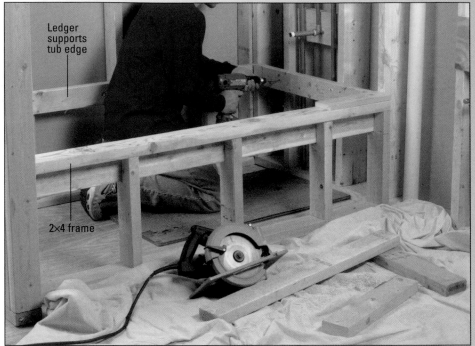

Ledger supports tub edge

2×4 frame

1 Build a frame following manufacturers directions. It's especially important to get the height right. You may snug the whirlpool up against one, two, or three walls. Where you snug the tub against the wall, attach a 2×4 ledger as you would for a standard tub *(page 49)*. Where you will install tiles, plan the framing carefully, taking into account the thickness of the backerboard (Steps 2 and 11). Most whirlpools require access to the plumbing at one end and the pump motor at the other end; check the manufacturer's directions.

WHIRLPOOL TUB INSTALLATION

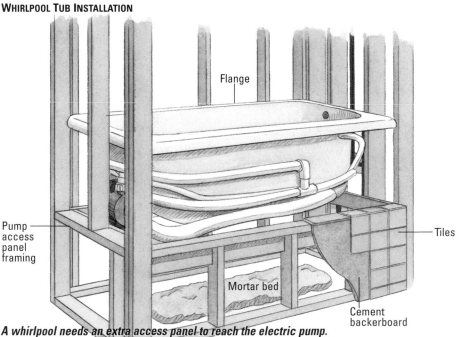

Flange

Pump access panel framing

Tiles

Mortar bed

Cement backerboard

A whirlpool needs an extra access panel to reach the electric pump. A 2×4 frame is covered with backerboard, then tiled. The whirlpool's flange rests on tile, but its weight must be supported by a mortar bed.

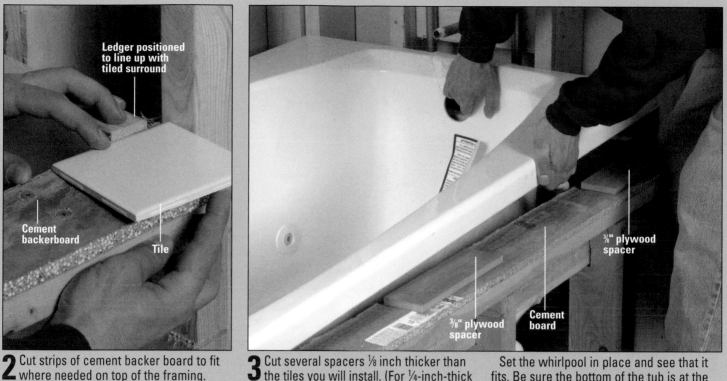

2 Cut strips of cement backer board to fit where needed on top of the framing. Backerboard pieces should overhang the framing by ½ inch. You can also cut the side backer board pieces but don't install them yet. Attach the backer board using special backer board screws.

3 Cut several spacers ⅛ inch thicker than the tiles you will install. (For ¼-inch-thick tiles, cut pieces of ⅜-inch plywood.) Set the spacers on top of the backerboard wherever there will be tile.

Set the whirlpool in place and see that it fits. Be sure the bottom of the tub is at the correct depth so it will rest on the mortar bed (Steps 7 and 8).

Installing a GFCI (ground fault circuit interrupter) receptacle

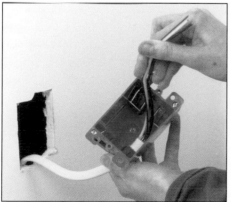

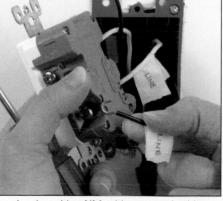

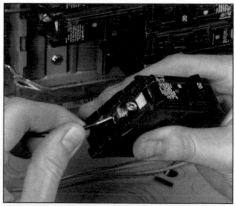

Most whirlpools plug into a GFCI receptacle, though some are hard-wired into an electrical box. For most models, you will need a 15-amp circuit that supplies only the whirlpool. Check the manufacturer's instructions. Consult with an electrician if you are not sure how to run cable and install a new circuit. Use cable that meets local codes; either NM cable, armored cable, or conduit with wires running through it. Run cable from the service panel to the whirlpool. Strip the cable and clamp it to an electrical box (left).

Wire a GFCI receptacle (center), wrap the connections, secure the receptacle in the box, and attach a cover plate.

Shut off power to the service panel. Strip the cable and connect the hot wire to a new electrical breaker (right). Connect the neutral and ground wires to the neutral and/or ground bus bar and snap the breaker into place. Restore power and test.

Installing a whirlpool tub (continued)

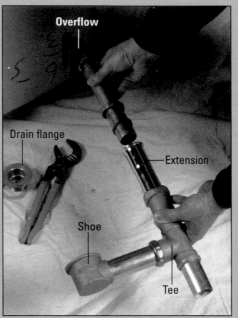

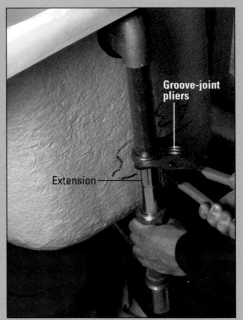

4 Check to make sure the drain trap is positioned and at the correct height so that the whirlpool waste-and-overflow unit will slide into it (Step 9). Plan how you will make this connection, either from the basement or crawlspace below or through the access panel *(page 51)*.

5 Assemble the waste-and-overflow unit. Some whirlpools come with a waste-and-overflow; if not you'll have to purchase a standard unit and add an extension (shown). Insert the shoe (cut to length if necessary) into the tee fitting.

6 Set the tub on two overturned buckets. Install the overflow by slipping in the plunger assembly, tightening the screws on the cover plate, and screwing the drain flange into the shoe (see *pages 50–51)*. Tighten the nuts on the drain extension.

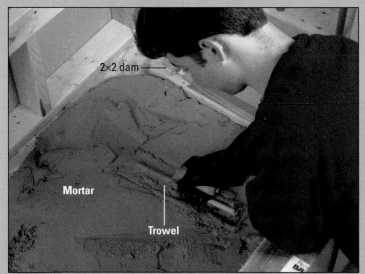

7 Test-fit the whirlpool to see that the waste-and-overflow unit will slip into the drain trap. Remove the whirlpool. Screw 2×2s to the floor around the drain hole to keep mortar out of the hole. In a bucket or wheelbarrow, mix water with dry mortar mix. The mortar should be just wet enough to be poured. Smooth enough mortar onto the floor to support the bottom of the whirlpool.

8 Place spacers (Step 3) on the backer board atop the side-panel frame. With a helper, gently set the tub in place. Guide the waste-and-overflow into the drain trap but do not tighten the connection. Push down on the tub until the lip just rests on the spacers, but do not press hard. Allow the mortar to harden overnight.

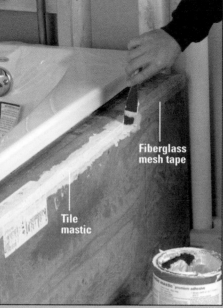

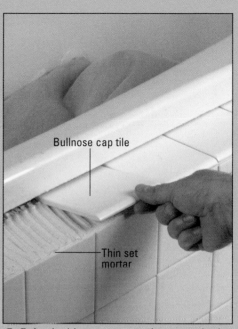

9 Connect the waste-and-overflow to the drain and tighten the fittings *(pages 50–51)*. Support the pump motor with pieces of lumber and attach it in place with screws. Plug the cord into the GFCI receptacle. Follow manufacturer's instructions for testing the whirlpool.

10 Install cement backer board on all exposed sides. Drive backer board screws every 6 inches or so. Wrap corners with fiberglass mesh tape.

11 Apply thinset mortar using a notched trowel and set standard tiles on the side. When tiling the top edge, use bullnose caps for the outside corner for a finished look. After the thinset has dried, apply grout and clean the joints. Caulk the joint where the whirlpool rests on the tiles.

Adding the tub hardware

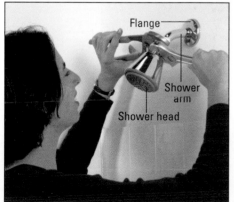

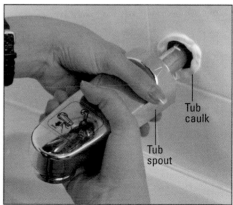

1 Once the wall is finished, remove the temporary nipple. Wrap pipe-thread tape around the ends of the shower arm and screw it into place. Slip on the flange. Twist on the shower head, then tighten with an adjustable wrench and groove-joint pliers. Protect the chrome with tape.

2 Following manufacturer's instructions, slide the escutcheon over the faucet and screw it into place. It should seal against the tiles with a rubber gasket. Attach the faucet handle.

3 Apply caulk around the spout hole. Choose a nipple of proper length for the spout and wrap pipe-thread tape around the threads of both ends. Twist the spout on by hand. Finish by wrapping the spout with a rag and tightening it against the wall with groove-joint pliers.

CONNECTING THE TOILET AND SINK

Once the rough plumbing is completed, run electrical lines and install the lights, switches, receptacles, and a ceiling fan. Lay the finish flooring if you haven't already done so. Install cement backer board on the walls that surround the tub/shower (pages 56–57) and moisture-resistant drywall (also called greenboard) on the other walls. Tile or apply prefab sheets to the tub/shower surround. Tape, prime, and paint the walls and the ceiling. You may want to install baseboard and trim, but often it's best to wait until the sink and toilet are installed to avoid bumps and nicks.

To install stop valves for the toilet and the sink, follow the instructions on *page 77*. Measure the lengths of the supply tubes needed and confirm the connection dimensions.

PRESTART CHECKLIST

☐ **TIME**
Most of a day to install a toilet, pedestal sink, and sink faucet

☐ **TOOLS**
Adjustable wrench, groove-joint pliers, torpedo level, screwdriver, basin wrench, drill

☐ **SKILLS**
Assembling plumbing parts, cementing PVC fittings

☐ **PREP**
Finish all the wiring, carpentry, and wall preparation; remove the drop cloth from the floor.

☐ **MATERIALS**
Toilet, wax ring, toilet flange with bolts, supply tubes and decorative flanges for sink and toilet, sink, sink bracket, bathroom faucet (with pop-up assembly), plumber's putty, silicone sealant, caulk, PVC primer and glue

Installing a toilet

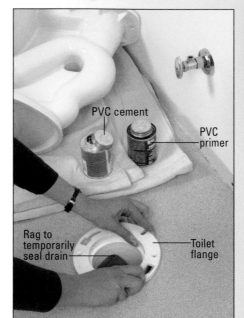
PVC cement
PVC primer
Rag to temporarily seal drain
Toilet flange

1 Install finish flooring to within an inch of the drain hole. The toilet flange can rest on top of the finished floor or on top of the subflooring. Test-fit the flange, then prime and glue it so that you will be able to place the hold-down bolts on either side of the opening (Step 2). Remove the rag.

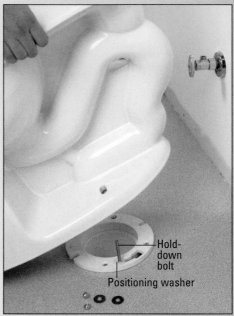
Hold-down bolt
Positioning washer

2 Press a wax ring onto the bottom of the toilet. Place the hold-down bolts in the flange and slip plastic positioning washers over them. Lower the bowl, threading the bolts through the holes in the bowl. Press down to seat the bowl firmly. Slip on washers and nuts and gently tighten.

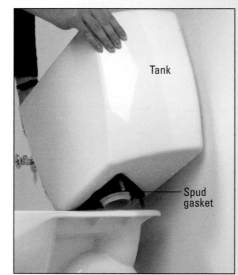
Tank
Spud gasket

3 Assemble the tank and the bowl of a new toilet following the manufacturer's instructions. A large spud gasket seals the opening below the flush-valve seat. Place a rubber washer under the head of each mounting bolt. Don't over tighten the nuts.

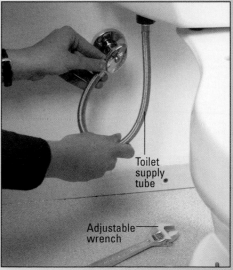
Toilet supply tube
Adjustable wrench

4 Attach a toilet supply tube by hand-tightening the nuts at the underside of the tank and the stop valve. Tighten a half turn or more with a wrench and open the stop valve. You may need to tighten a connection a bit further.

Installing a sink

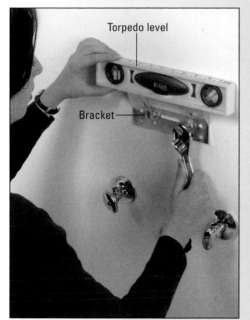

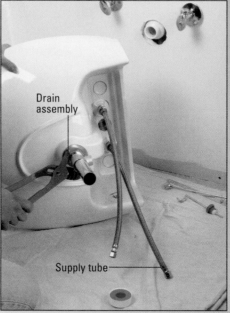

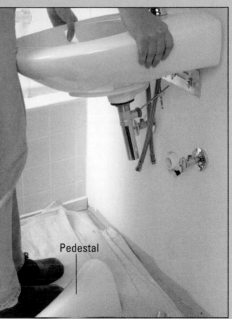

1 A pedestal sink must rest on a bracket that is firmly screwed to a brace inside the wall (Step 2, *page 90*). Temporarily set the sink on the pedestal, slip it into place, and mark for the correct bracket height. Remove the sink and install the bracket with two or three lag screws and washers.

2 Set the sink on its side, padded by a drop cloth. Install the faucet. Connect the sink trap, select supply tubes (see *page 18*) and connect them.

3 Set the sink on the bracket and make sure the pedestal can slide in; you may need to adjust the height of the bracket. Hook up the trap and supply tubes. Slide the pedestal into place. On some models, the pedestal must be screwed to the floor.

Installing a vanity sink base

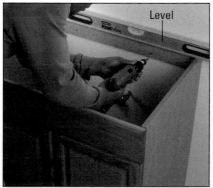

You may need to cut holes in the back of a vanity base cabinet for the plumbing. Slide the cabinet into place and check it for level in both directions. If necessary slip shims under the bottom or behind the back of the cabinet. Drive screws through the cabinet framing into wall studs to secure the cabinet.

WHAT IF...
You want a freestanding bowl sink?

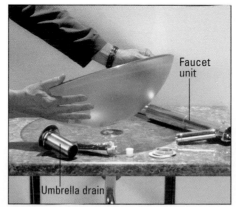

1 Drill two holes in the top, one for the drain and one for the faucet. There is no overflow, so use an umbrella drain (shown) to cover the drain. Apply silicone sealant and anchor by tightening the nut from below.

2 Anchor the faucet by tightening a nut and leveling screws from below. This faucet comes with flexible supply tubes that connect directly to the stop valves. Make a tailpiece from a section of trap and attach it with a rubber washer and trap nut.

Installing Kitchen Plumbing

Rough plumbing for a typical kitchen is much simpler than for a bathroom. Assuming there will be one sink and one dishwasher, only one drain line and one pair of supply pipes will be needed. All other connections—the drain and supply for the dishwasher, a supply line for an icemaker, and even a hot-water dispenser or a water filter—are made with flexible rubber or copper tubing that does not run through walls.

The finish plumbing, however, can get complicated. The underside of a typical kitchen sink may look like a bewildering maze of tubes, appliances, and trap lines.

This chapter eliminates the confusion by taking things one step at a time.

The master plan

Remodeling a kitchen involves many different operations. Usually, the most efficient order of work is the following:

■ Cover sensitive surfaces and remove old cabinets, flooring, and wall coverings.

■ Install the rough plumbing—the drain, vent, and supply lines.

■ Install electrical wiring and boxes and cut a hole for an exhaust fan, if included.

■ Apply new drywall and patch any damaged walls. Prime and paint.

■ Install the flooring, then cover it with a protective drop cloth.

■ Install the wall and base cabinets, as well as the countertops.

■ Do the finish electrical work—lights, receptacles, switches.

■ Install the sink, faucet, garbage disposer, dishwasher, and any other plumbing appliances.

For more help on remodeling tasks other than plumbing see books in the Stanley series such as Basic Wiring, Advanced Wiring, Basic Tiling, and Interior Walls.

Rough plumbing for a kitchen is simple, but the finish installation calls for patient, methodical work.

Chapter Preview

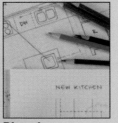
Planning a kitchen
page 102

Running drain lines
page 104

Extending supply lines
page 106

Preparing the cabinets
page 108

Any horizontal run of the revent must be at least 6 inches above the "flood level" of the sink—the rim of the sink. In this case, window framing is only a couple of inches above the countertop so a diagonal run of vent is needed. This prevents debris from settling in the vent should the sink back up.

If the drain line must travel more than 6 feet to reach the stack, you'll probably need to run the drain down through the floor and connect to the stack in the room below.

Sometimes it's easiest to dry-fit all or part of the drain and vent runs and then make the marks for cutting existing pipes and drilling holes. Use a level to check the vent and drain lines for correct slope—¼ inch per running foot. Fasten the dry run in place with duct tape. This allows you to accurately mark for tying into the stack. In addition, you can double-check slope and the final location of the drain stubout.

Hooking up the sink
page 110

Installing a dishwasher
page 114

PLANNING A KITCHEN

Many kitchen remodeling projects do not require new rough-in work. If the new sink is closer than 3 feet from an existing drain line, you can probably reach it by simply extending the trap. If supply lines need only to move over a few feet, you can probably attach a tee to one of the existing lines and route the new lines through cabinets, rather than inside walls. In this case, you may not need a plumbing permit; but check with your local building department to be sure.

The plan shown here calls for the standard trio of kitchen plumbing appliances— a double-bowl sink, a garbage disposer, and a dishwasher. Other appliances, such as a water filter *(page 71)* or a hot-water dispenser, can be added without much trouble either during the initial installation or sometime later. A pot-filler faucet *(page 112)*, however, requires pipes that run through walls.

The drain and vent line

The sink trap connects to the sanitary tee of a 2-inch drain line. The ideal height of the tee varies depending on the depth of the sink. (If the tee is lower than the ideal height, you can simply extend the trap downward. If the tee is too high, you may need to install a new tee at a lower point.)

The drain line must be properly vented; see *pages 10–11.* Often, the kitchen drain is connected to a separate stack, smaller in diameter than the main stack, which extends up all the way out the roof. It's also possible to revent the drain line. Because kitchens are usually on the first floor, a revent line in a two-story house may need to travel up to the second floor or even to the attic.

Lots of grease gets poured down a kitchen sink. In many older homes, the kitchen drainpipe leads to an outside catch basin, which can be accessed periodically in order to scoop out the grease. If your system has no catch basin (or grease trap), at least be sure there is an easily accessible cleanout.

This plan calls for a cleanout located just below the sanitary tee.

The supply lines

The hot-water pipe supplies the faucet and the dishwasher; there should be a stop.

KITCHEN PLUMBING OVERVIEW

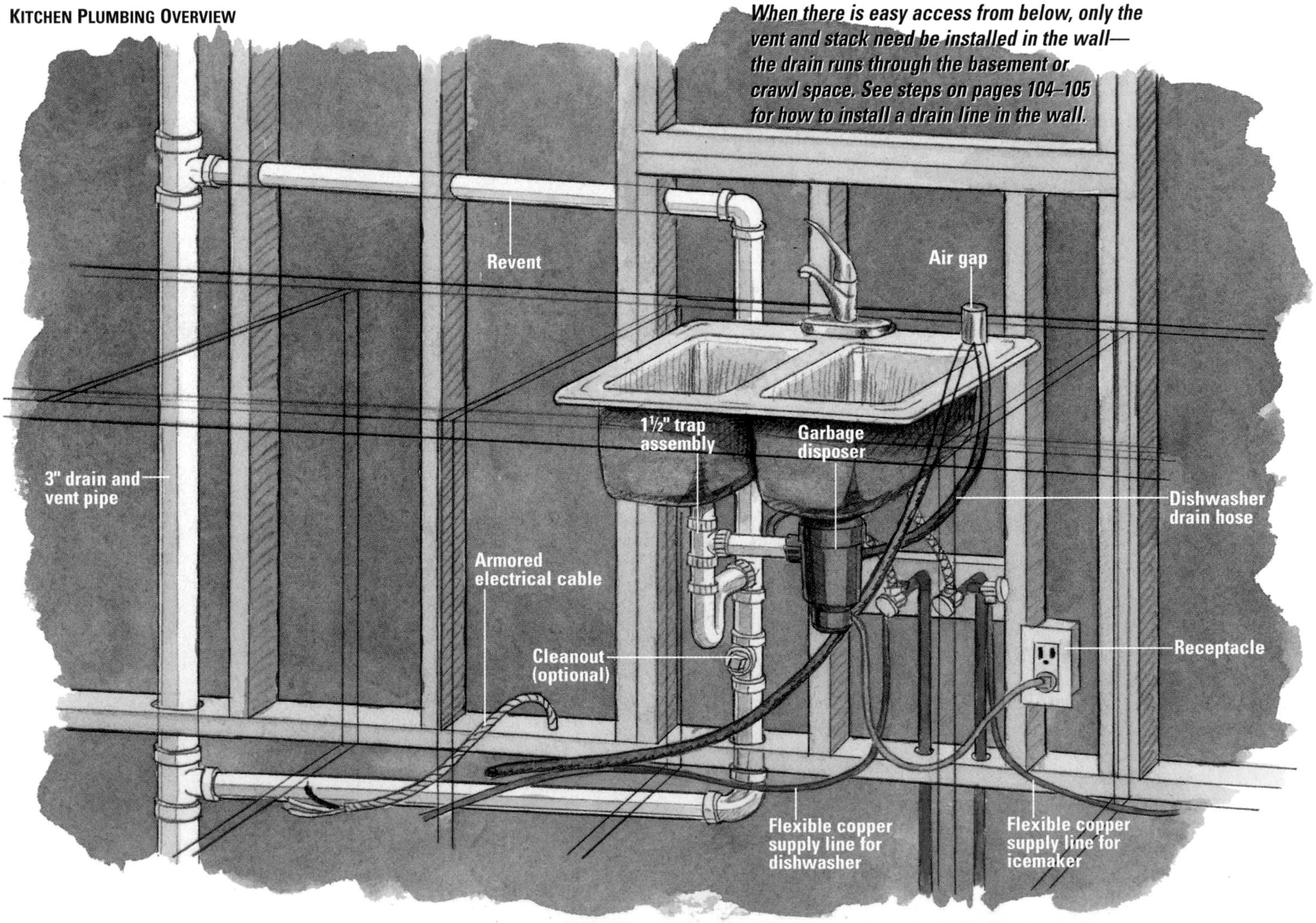

When there is easy access from below, only the vent and stack need be installed in the wall— the drain runs through the basement or crawl space. See steps on pages 104–105 for how to install a drain line in the wall.

Revent

Air gap

3" drain and vent pipe

1½" trap assembly

Garbage disposer

Dishwasher drain hose

Armored electrical cable

Cleanout (optional)

Receptacle

Flexible copper supply line for dishwasher

Flexible copper supply line for icemaker

valve for each. The cold-water pipe supplies the faucet as well as a line that runs to the icemaker; there is a stop valve for each.

The sink, cabinets, and countertop
The window above a kitchen sink is typically 42 inches high, so any vent lines must be installed to either side of the window. A standard base cabinet topped with a countertop is 36 inches high. A special "sink base" cabinet has no drawers or shelves to make room for the sink and the plumbing.

A hole must be cut in the countertop to accommodate the sink *(page 110).* You can do this yourself if the countertop is plastic laminate. If the top is granite or solid-surface, hire a pro to cut the top.

Usually the dishwasher is positioned right next to the sink base to simplify running the drain and supply line. (It is also the most convenient location for doing the dishes.) A 24-inch-wide opening houses a standard dishwasher.

Drawing a kitchen plan
On a piece of graph paper, draw a top view showing all the appliances, cabinets, electrical receptacles, and lights. Be precise, because every inch counts in a kitchen. A home center or kitchen supply source may have a computer program that will help you visualize possible layouts.

Kitchen designers often speak of a "work triangle," meaning that the sink, range, and refrigerator should all be within easy reach. This is easily accomplished in a kitchen that is U-shaped. If the kitchen is long and narrow, it's usually best to place one of the three elements on the wall opposite the other two. Make sure you can open the refrigerator without interfering with cooking or washing dishes.

Place the range at least 12 inches away from the sink. And leave 36 inches of counter space on either side of the sink for food preparation and draining dishes.

Most people prefer the sink to be placed in front of a window. The range should have a range hood above it, and the hood should vent to the outside.

If you plan to move or remove a wall, first check with a carpenter to make sure it's not load-bearing. If it is, you may be able to install a beam in its place.

Make drawings *(pages 26–27)* to refine your plans and prepare for permit application. If you are tying into a waste-vent-drain system with other fixtures, see the chart on *page 25* to confirm drain and supply pipe sizes. Start with a floorplan (above right), then settle specifics with a DWV (drain-waste-vent) elevation.

STANLEY PRO TIP

Standard specs

Check local codes for all pipe sizes and other dimensions. Here are some standard specs:

Drain and vent pipes
Sink: 2-inch drain; 1½- or 2-inch vent
Stack: 2 inches or larger
Sink drain: 18 inches above floor

Supply pipes
Faucet: ½-inch pipe
Faucet stubouts: Locate them where they can be easily reached once the sink is installed.

Other fittings
Include stop valves on the hot-water line for the dishwasher and sink. Include stop valves on the cold-water supply for the sink and lines for other appliances such as an icemaker or hot-water dispenser.

RUNNING DRAIN LINES

If you need to run a new drainpipe, draw a simple plan, showing how it will be vented and where it will connect to the house's drain. Have your plan approved by a local plumbing inspector.

Because it needs to house only a 2-inch drain/vent pipe, a kitchen usually does not have an extra-thick "wet wall," as does a bathroom. Kitchen plumbing is sometimes run through an exterior wall; in that case, make sure the pipes are well insulated. In areas with cold winters, it is best to run supply pipes up from the basement through the floor rather than through the wall.

Remove all cabinets that are in the way; they are surprisingly easy to remove. Completely cover all cabinets and flooring that you will reuse to protect them from scratches.

If wiring is in the way, **shut off the power to the circuit** and test to make sure power is off. You may want to remove a cable before working on the drain.

See *pages 40–43* for how to run pipes through walls and connect to existing pipes.

PRESTART CHECKLIST

☐ **TIME**
About a day to run a new drain line with a revent

☐ **TOOLS**
PVC saw or circular saw, level, drill with hole saw, reciprocating saw, layout square

☐ **SKILLS**
Cutting and joining PVC pipe, running pipes through walls, connecting new pipe to old

☐ **PREP**
Clear the room of all obstructions. Have your plans approved by an inspector.

☐ **MATERIALS**
PVC pipe and fittings to suit local codes, fitting for joining to the drainpipe, PVC primer and cement, pipe straps

1 Once you've put together a dry run of the drain and vent lines *(page 101)*, mark for cutting holes in the framing. Using a layout square, strike a line even with the top of the pipe. Then mark for the center of the pipe at the center of the stud.

2 For running 2-inch pipe, use a 2½-inch hole saw to drill through the studs (see *pages 84–89*). When possible, cut until the guide bit pierces the stud, then cut from the opposite side. Assemble the pipes in the wall, notching the studs where necessary.

INSTALLING A KITCHEN DRAIN-WASTER-VENT SYSTEM

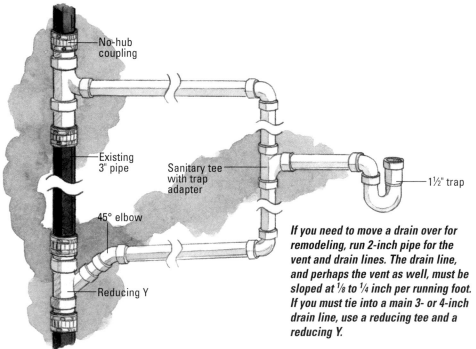

If you need to move a drain over for remodeling, run 2-inch pipe for the vent and drain lines. The drain line, and perhaps the vent as well, must be sloped at ⅛ to ¼ inch per running foot. If you must tie into a main 3- or 4-inch drain line, use a reducing tee and a reducing Y.

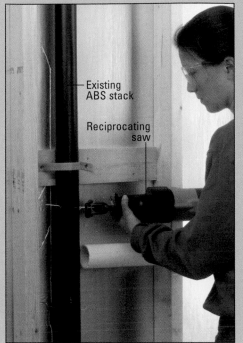

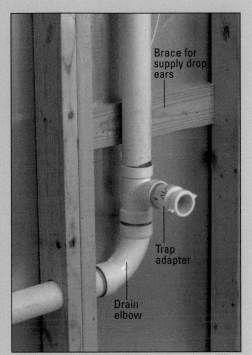

3 Having used the dry run to mark the existing stack *(page 101)*, add braces and pipe straps to stabilize the drain. If the stack is cast iron, see *pages 38–39* for how to support it. Then cut away a section to make way for the new installation.

4 If the stack is ABS (shown) or cast iron, use short lengths of PVC pipe and no-hub fittings to connect a sanitary tee for the vent and a Y and 45-degree street elbow for the drain. Then mark and cut a section of 2-inch PVC pipe to complete the stack.

5 Install a brace for the supply drop ears. Mark, prime, and cement *(pages 32–33)* the drain-vent system.

WHAT IF...
You install a sink in an island?

A sink installed in a kitchen island poses a special problem because there is no easy way to tie into a vent. The solution is a loop vent. This is a complicated setup, so consult with an inspector after you draw up your plans.

The drainpipe is run in the standard manner—a 1½-inch trap linking up 2-inch sink drain that runs down to a 3- or 4-inch drainpipe by means of a sanitary tee.

The vent pipe first loops up as high as possible, then runs down and over to a suitable vent pipe run up a wall. Because some water will likely enter the vent pipe, it must also be connected to the drainpipe using a sanitary tee fitting.

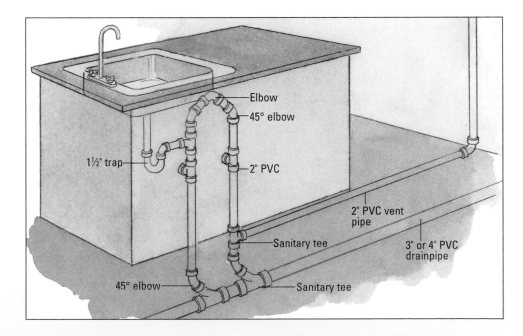

EXTENDING SUPPLY LINES

In a typical kitchen setup, hot and cold supply lines emerge from the wall just below the sink faucet, where they are connected to stop valves. Supply pipes should run inside walls rather than through cabinets to keep them safe from harm.

Because pipes under a sink are liable to get bumped, these pages show the most durable installation for the emerging pipes, using drop-ear elbows and galvanized nipples.

Half-inch rigid copper pipe is large enough for most kitchen installations. (For information on how to cut and join copper supply pipe, see *pages 30–31.*)

These pages show separate stop valves for the hot and cold faucet lines, the dishwasher, and an icemaker. If you want to add a water filter, hot-water dispenser, or other appliance, you may need additional stop valves. Saddle tee valves, which simply tap into a pipe, are easy to install but are prone to clogging.

PRESTART CHECKLIST

☐ **TIME**
Several hours to run copper supply lines through a floor or wall

☐ **TOOLS**
Drill, level, combination square, propane torch, groove-joint pliers, C-clamps

☐ **SKILLS**
Cutting and joining copper pipe, running pipe through walls or floors

☐ **PREP**
Install the drain line and carefully plan the location of the supply lines. **Shut off the water** before beginning work.

☐ **MATERIALS**
Copper pipe and fittings, galvanized nipples and tees, stop valves, flux, solder, nailing plates, shims

1 Where possible, run pipes through the centers of studs. Use a level or other long straightedge to mark for straight runs from stud to stud and use a combination square to mark for the center of studs. Drill ¾-inch holes to accommodate ½-inch pipe.

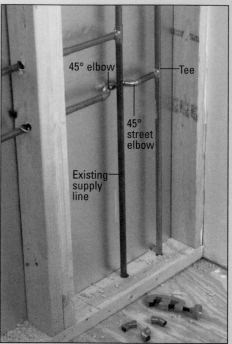

2 Shut off water and drain the lines you will tap into. Cut the existing pipes and install new tee fittings *(page 43).* If you must run around a pipe or other obstruction, use 45-degree elbows and street elbows.

STANLEY PRO TIP

Choosing the right stop valve

Make sure each stop valve is the right size and type for both the pipe and the supply tube that it will attach to. A kitchen stop valve should have a ½-inch outlet.

If you will be joining to rigid copper pipe (rather than a brass nipple as shown above), buy a valve that sweats onto the pipe *(page 30),* or one that joins with compression fittings (upper right).

If the pipe rises vertically through the floor, use a straight stop valve (lower left), rather than an angle stop.

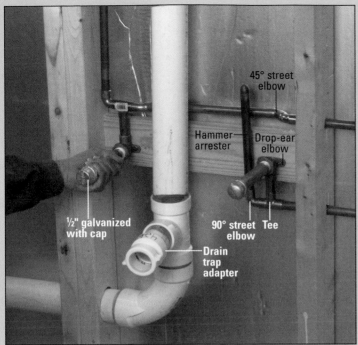

45° street elbow

Hammer arrester

Drop-ear elbow

½" galvanized with cap

90° street elbow

Tee

Drain trap adapter

C-clamp

3 Usually, the most convenient location for stubouts is on each side of the drain trap adapter, as shown. However, feel free to place them wherever they will be within easy reach but within 18 inches of the faucet inlets. At each stubout, install a hammer arrester and a drop-ear elbow. Do a dry run (shown), then sweat the fittings and reattach the drop-ears to the braces. Add nipples with caps; turn on the water and check for leaks.

4 Install the wall covering, prime and paint the walls, and install the flooring. Install the kitchen base cabinets. Plumb and level them and attach them to each other (shown) and to the walls. If the sink base has a back, you'll need to drill holes for the stubouts.

WHAT IF...
Supply lines run beneath the floor?

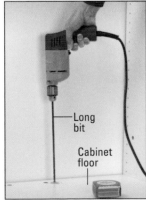

Long bit

Cabinet floor

To run pipes up through the floor from a basement below, install the cabinet first. Use a long drill bit to bore a locator hole down through the cabinet and into the space below.

ELECTRICAL CONNECTION FOR GARBAGE DISPOSER AND HOT-WATER DISPENSER

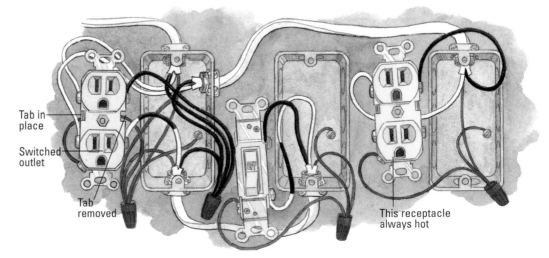

Tab in place

Switched outlet

Tab removed

This receptacle always hot

A garbage disposer should be plugged into a receptacle that is controlled by a switch. In the circuit illustrated above, a separate receptacle is always *hot, so you can plug in an appliance such as a hot-water dispenser. Shut off power before running wires and make sure that the new appliances will* *not overload the circuit. Consult with an electrician if you are not completely sure of doing the job yourself.*

PREPARING THE CABINETS

Once the drain and supply pipes have been installed and tested for leaks, run any electrical lines for receptacles and lights. Cover the walls with drywall, and prime and paint. Install the finish flooring, then protect it with cardboard or heavy paper and a drop cloth.

Purchase the sink , garbage disposer, dishwasher, and any other appliances. Unpack them and check the manufacturers' literature for the installation requirements. In particular, be sure about the dimensions of the opening for the dishwasher, as well as the size and location of the hole for its drain and supply lines.

A sink base cabinet has no drawers or shelves to leave room for all the appliances, tubes, and pipes that must fit inside it. Some sink bases are actual completed cabinets, while others consist of only the face and the floor.

PRESTART CHECKLIST

☐ **TIME**
A full day to install kitchen cabinets; plus several hours to run the electrical line for the dishwasher

☐ **TOOLS**
Hammer, drill, level, groove-joint pliers, adjustable wrench

☐ **SKILLS**
Measuring, drilling, and sawing accurately to install cabinets that are level and properly spaced

☐ **PREP**
Run and test all the rough plumbing.

☐ **MATERIALS**
Cabinets, shims, screws, tees, close nipples, pipe-thread tape, stop valves, 14/2 armored cable

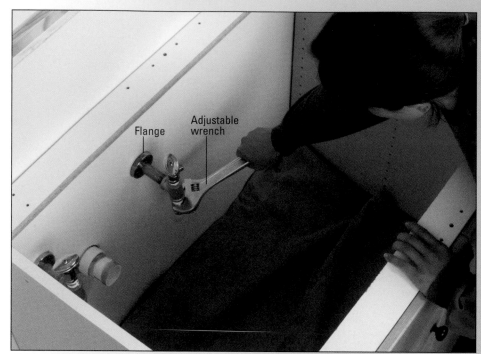

Flange   Adjustable wrench

1 **Shut off the water,** and drain the line. For each supply, remove the cap from the nipple and slide on a flange to cover the hole at the wall. Wrap the nipple threads with pipe-thread tape, and install a tee. Wrap Teflon tape around the threads of two short nipples, and screw them into the tee fitting. Screw stop valves onto the nipples. Turn the valve handles off, and restore water pressure to test for leaks.

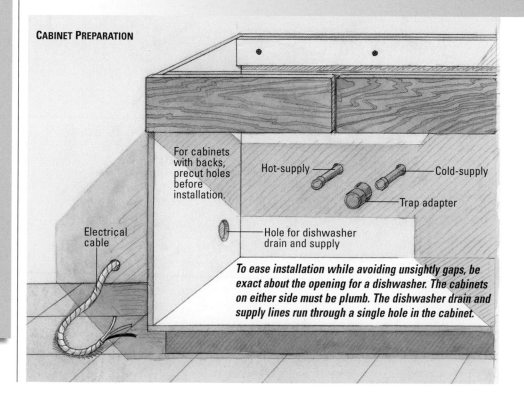

CABINET PREPARATION

For cabinets with backs, precut holes before installation.

Hot-supply

Cold-supply

Trap adapter

Electrical cable

Hole for dishwasher drain and supply

To ease installation while avoiding unsightly gaps, be exact about the opening for a dishwasher. The cabinets on either side must be plumb. The dishwasher drain and supply lines run through a single hole in the cabinet.

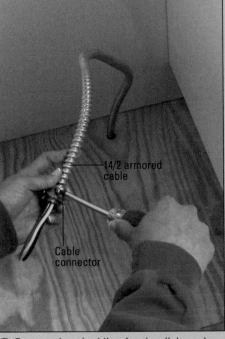

2 The dishwasher opening should be 24¼ inches wide for most models; check manufacturer's instructions. If installing a cabinet to the other side of the dishwasher (shown above), level from the sink base cabinet, plumb, and fasten it in place.

3 Run an electrical line for the dishwasher. Usually, a 14/2 armored cable connected to a 15-amp circuit is sufficient, but check codes and the manufacturer's literature. Be certain that the dishwasher will not overload the circuit. **Hire an electrician if you are not sure of your wiring abilities.**

4 The dishwasher instructions will tell you the best place to drill a hole for running the drain and supply lines. Usually a single 1½-inch hole is sufficient.

Cutting countertop for a sink

To cut a laminate countertop for a sink, place the new sink upside down on top of the countertop, centered over the base cabinet. Trace around the sink, then draw another line ¾ inch inside the first line. Cut along the second line using a saber saw equipped with a fine-cutting blade.

Choosing a sink

When it comes to sink materials, you generally get what you pay for. An inexpensive stainless-steel sink flexes when you push on it, scratches easily, and is difficult to keep clean. A higher-quality heavy-gauge (6- or 8-gauge) stainless-steel sink, such as one with a burnished finish, is a better choice. When choosing a stainless-steel sink, make sure the underside is well coated with sound-deadening insulation.

An enameled cast-iron sink comes in a variety of colors. It lasts much longer than an enameled steel sink. Acrylic sinks (like the one shown) have the look of enameled cast iron, and the higher-end models are nearly as durable. Both cast-iron and acrylic sinks have insulating properties so that water stays warm in them longer than it does in a stainless-steel sink.

Stainless steel

Heavy-gauge stainless steel

Cast iron

Acrylic

HOOKING UP THE SINK

Once you have cut the hole in the countertop *(page 109),* set the sink into the hole to make sure it will fit.

It is possible to install the sink first and then attach the faucet, garbage disposer, and drain from below. However, you'll save yourself hassle and time if you connect most of the components to the sink before installing it. Spread a drop cloth on the countertop nearby and set the sink upside down on the cloth. The faucet holes should overhang the counter so you can install the faucet. Or better yet, set the sink on two sawhorses, padded with rags or towels.

Enameled-steel (shown) and stainless-steel sinks clamp to the countertop with special clips that are usually included with the sink. Test to make sure that the clips will work on your countertop before you install the plumbing. A cast-iron sink is heavy enough that it needs no clips.

PRESTART CHECKLIST

☐ **TIME**
About half a day to install a sink with disposer and dishwasher connections

☐ **TOOLS**
Drill, screwdriver, groove-joint pliers, adjustable wrench, strainer wrench or spud wrench

☐ **SKILLS**
Connecting a trap, installing a faucet and garbage disposer

☐ **PREP**
Install the rough plumbing, a switched receptacle, and the cabinets.

☐ **MATERIALS**
Sink, faucet, garbage disposer, appliance extension cord, wire nuts, trap assembly, supply tubes, flexible copper line for dishwasher and icemaker supplies, drain hose (usually included with the dishwasher), air gap, plumber's putty, drop cloth

1 Install a standard basket strainer in one sink hole, and the garbage disposer strainer in the other hole. Make sure you know which strainer goes to which hole. Place a rope of putty under the lip of the strainer body and hold it in place as you slip on the washers and tighten the nut.

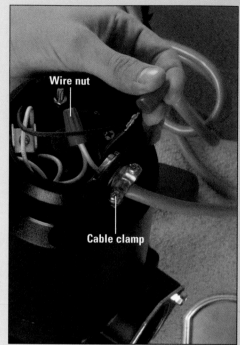

2 Following manufacturer's instructions, dismantle the garbage disposer mounting hardware. Open the electrical coverplate and hook up an appliance extension cord using wire nuts. Replace the coverplate.

SINK ASSEMBLY

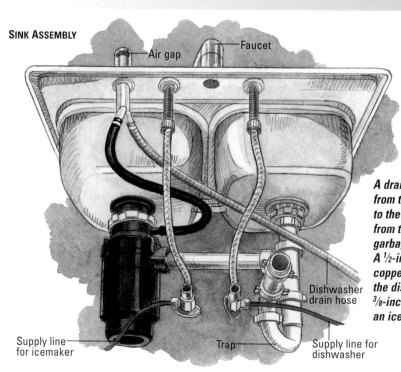

A drain hose runs from the dishwasher to the air gap and from there to the garbage disposer. A ¹/₂-inch flexible copper line supplies the dishwasher; a ³/₈-inch line supplies an icemaker.

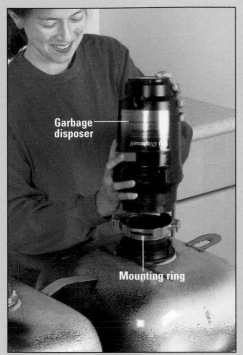

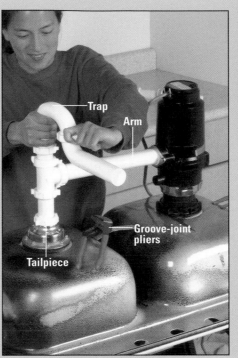

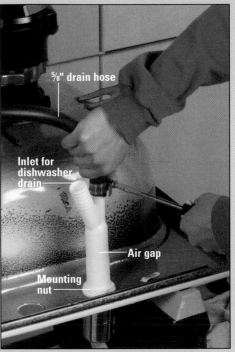

3 Slide the garbage disposer mount ring over the flange and then install the cushion mount, making sure the groove on the inside fits over the lip of the sink flange. Position the disposer over the flange; push down and twist until the disposer is fully anchored.

4 Assemble the drain trap. Begin by installing the tailpiece and the arm that attaches to the disposer. Cut pieces to size as needed, then install the trap. Set the sink in the hole to see whether the trap lines up with the trap adapter in the wall; you may need to trim a piece or add an extension.

5 Attach the air gap with a mounting nut. Run a ⅝-inch hose from the air gap to the disposer. Secure the hose with hose clamps. If the drain hose is easily disconnected from the dishwasher, attach it to the air gap now. Otherwise attach it when you install the dishwasher *(page 115).*

ALTERNATE TRAP CONFIGURATIONS

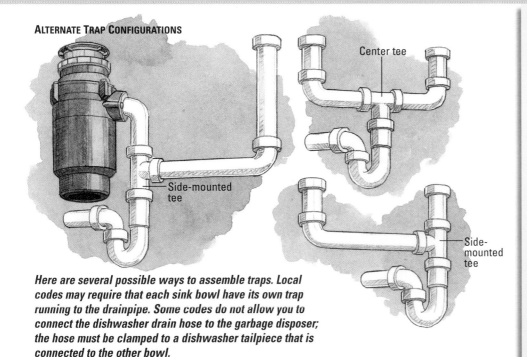

Here are several possible ways to assemble traps. Local codes may require that each sink bowl have its own trap running to the drainpipe. Some codes do not allow you to connect the dishwasher drain hose to the garbage disposer; the hose must be clamped to a dishwasher tailpiece that is connected to the other bowl.

STANLEY PRO TIP

Assembling a trap

When connecting the pieces of a chrome or PVC trap, don't forget the slip nut and washer for each joint. Where a tailpiece attaches to a strainer, a special type of washer may be used. You'll probably need to cut at least one pipe; use a hacksaw or a fine-toothed saw (for PVC only) and a miter box.

HOOKING UP THE SINK (continued)

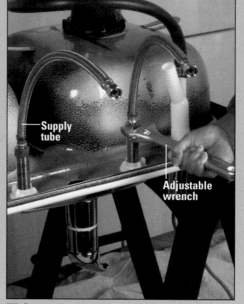

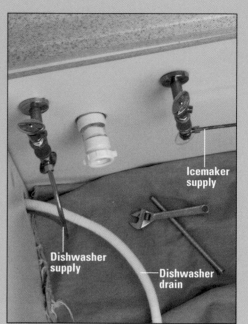

6 Install the faucet. If the faucet does not come with a plastic or rubber gasket, place a rope of putty under the faucet's flange to seal out water. Tighten the mounting hardware.

7 Screw flexible supply tubes onto the faucet inlets. Make sure their other ends are the right size to screw onto the stop valves. If the faucet has flexible copper inlets, use two adjustable wrenches to avoid kinking the inlets.

8 Before you set the sink into the hole, save yourself work later by hooking up as much plumbing as possible now. For instance, attach the supply lines for the dishwasher *(page 114)* and for the icemaker.

Installing a kettle-filler faucet

A faucet like this makes it easy to fill a large kettle while it is on the stove or countertop. This model supplies only cold water, but other types have cold and hot handles.

It is important to install the faucet firmly in the wall. Run a cold-water supply line up the wall. The last 2 feet or so should be extra-strong pipe, such as galvanized steel or brass. Install a threaded tee and a hammer arrester. Anchor a 2×6 or larger brace behind the pipe and the tee and attach the pipe and the tee using two-hole pipe straps.

Along with the faucet, buy a special inlet nipple, which has threads running all along its length in the same direction. A locking nut with washers allows you to screw the inlet nipple to the faucet at just the right depth so you can screw the faucet into the tee fitting at maximum tightness against the wall.

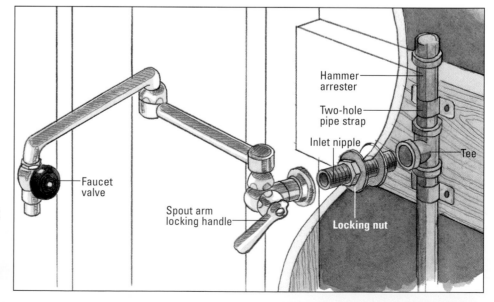

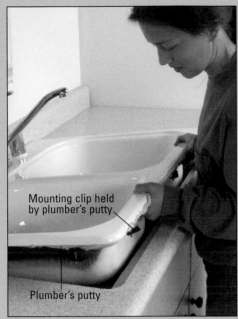

9 Place a rope of plumber's putty, thick enough to seal at all points, around the bottom lip of the sink. Position at least some of the mounting clips in the channels and hold them upright, using dabs of putty. Turn the sink right-side-up and carefully lower it into the hole.

10 From underneath, turn the clips so they grab the underside of the countertop. There should be a clip every 8 inches or so. Tighten each clip with a screwdriver or a drill equipped with a screwdriver bit.

11 Attach the trap to the trap adapter in the wall. Tighten all the connections with groove-joint pliers. To test, fill each bowl with water, then remove the stopper and watch for drips. Run the disposer with the water on and check for drips.

Installing a cast-iron sink

A cast-iron sink is very heavy, so have someone help you lift and position it. Apply a bead of silicone caulk around the hole. Carefully lower the sink into the opening. Avoid sliding it, which could compromise the caulk seal. Press down gently. Scrape away excess caulk with a plastic or wood scraper. Allow the caulk to set for several hours before attaching the plumbing.

Other sink installations

A flush-mounted or underhung sink makes for easier cleaning, but these require special countertop treatments.

Install a flush-mounted sink with its rim resting on plywood substrate. Install concrete backerboard around the sink and top it with tiles that partially rest on top of the sink flange.

Install and plumb an underhung sink after the substrate is installed. Then install tiles as shown, with thin vertical pieces around the perimeter and bullnose trim pieces overlapping them.

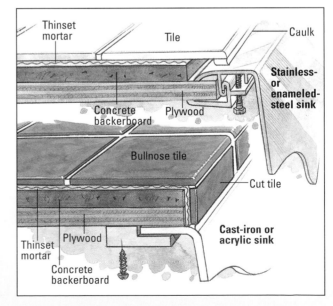

INSTALLING A DISHWASHER

Once you prepare the site correctly, installing a dishwasher is surprisingly easy. Make sure the opening is the correct size, and test-fit the dishwasher.

Run an electrical cable—preferably armored, though nonmetallic cable may be approved—into the space. Make sure it will not bump into the dishwasher's frame. In most cases, a 14/2 cable hooked to a 15-amp circuit will suffice. Make sure that hooking to the dishwasher will not overload the circuit. Check Stanley Advanced Wiring for more information. Hire an electrician if you are unsure of your abilities.

Most dishwashers come with a drain hose. The drain hose runs to an air gap mounted to a knockout hole in the sink *(page 112)*. From there, another length of hose runs to the garbage disposer. If there is no garbage disposer, it runs to a dishwasher tailpiece on the trap.

The water supply line is typically flexible copper, connected to its own shutoff valve. The cabinets on either side should be spaced according to manufacturer's instructions—usually 24¼ inches.

PRESTART CHECKLIST

☐ **TIME**
Once the electrical and plumbing lines are run and the cabinets installed, about an hour to install a dishwasher

☐ **TOOLS**
Tubing cutter, drill, screwdriver, adjustable wrench, groove-joint pliers

☐ **SKILLS**
Making simple plumbing and electrical connections

☐ **PREP**
Install the electrical and plumbing lines, as well as the cabinets and countertop.

☐ **MATERIALS**
Dishwasher with drain hose, hose clamps, air gap, flexible copper supply line, electrical cable, wire nuts

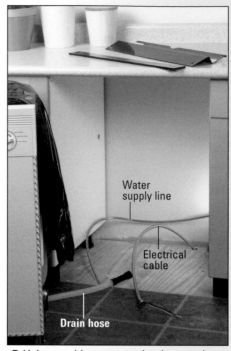

Water supply line

Electrical cable

Drain hose

1 Using a tubing cutter, trim the supply tube to the needed length. Check to make sure the electrical cable is long enough to reach the junction box built into the dishwasher.

Electrical cable

Water supply line

2 Push the dishwasher into the opening. As you do so, thread the drain line through the 1½-inch hole already cut in the cabinet. Make sure the lines do not become kinked or bent.

DISHWASHER CONNECTIONS

Three connections are needed for a dishwasher: An electrical cable supplies 120 volts of power; a drain line runs to the trap or garbage disposer; and a supply line, hooked to a stop valve under the sink, brings water to the dishwasher.

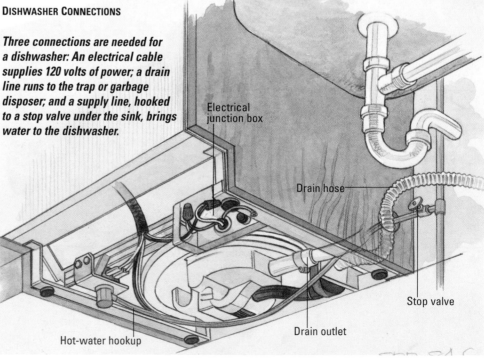

Electrical junction box

Drain hose

Stop valve

Drain outlet

Hot-water hookup

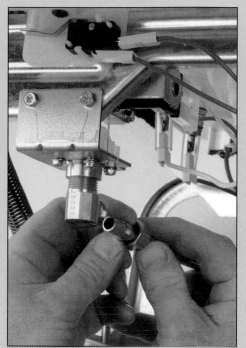

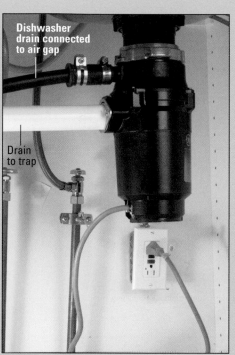

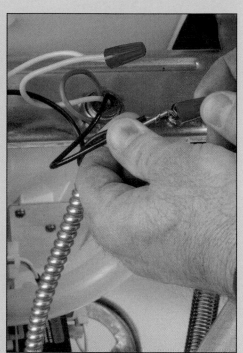

3 Slip a nut and ferrule onto the end of the supply line. Carefully bend the tubing and insert it into the supply inlet. Slide the ferrule down into the inlet and tighten the nut. Open the stop valve and check for leaks; you may need to tighten the nut further.

4 Run the drain line to the air gap, then to the garbage disposer or a tailpiece with a special dishwasher drain fitting. Slide a hose clamp onto the hose, slip the hose onto the fitting, slide the clamp over the fitting, and tighten the clamp.

5 Run the electrical cable through the cable clamp and tighten the clamp nuts to hold the cable firm. Strip and splice wires—black to black, white to white, and ground (green) to ground. Cap each splice with a wire nut and install the electrical coverplate.

Anchoring and leveling the dishwasher

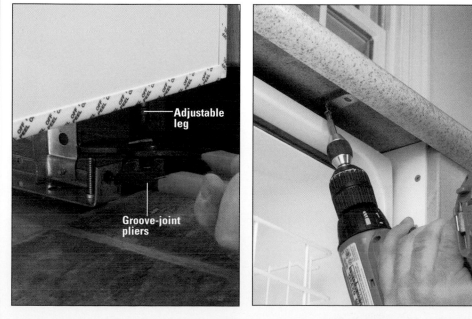

Slide the dishwasher in far enough so that only its decorative trim is visible. If the dishwasher won't go in far enough, pull it out and look for obstructions.

Stand back and check that the dishwasher looks straight in relation to the cabinets and the countertop. To raise or lower one or both sides, use groove-joint pliers to turn the feet at the bottom of the unit. Wiggle the dishwasher to test that it rests solidly on all four feet.

Once satisfied with the dishwasher's position, open the door and find the mounting tabs (usually on the top edge, sometimes on the sides). Drill pilot holes. To avoid drilling up through the countertop, wrap a piece of tape on the drill bit to mark the depth to stop at. Drive short screws into the holes to anchor the dishwasher to the countertop.

GLOSSARY

For terms not included here, or for more about those that are, refer to the index on *pages 118–120*.

ABS: One of the first plastic drain pipes used in homes. ABS (acrylonitrile-butadiene-styrene) is now forbidden in many municipalities in favor of PVC drainpipe.

Access panel: A removable panel in a wall or ceiling that permits repair or replacement of concealed items such as faucet bodies.

Adapter: A fitting that makes it possible to go from male endings to female endings or vice-versa. Transition adapters allow for joining different kinds of pipe together in the same run. Trap adapters help connect drainlines to a sink or lavatory trap.

Auger: A flexible metal cable fished into traps and drainlines to dislodge clogs.

Ballcock: The assembly inside a toilet tank that when activated releases water into the bowl to start the flushing action, then prepares the toilet for subsequent flushes. Also called a flush valve.

Basket strainer: A drain fitting on kitchen sinks that prevents debris from flowing into the drain and can be rotated so the sink can be filled.

Buffalo box: A type of whole-house shutoff where the valve is in a plastic or concrete box set in the ground.

CPVC: Heat-resistant and as strong as PVC, CPVC (chlorinated poly-vinyl-chloride) is approved by many municipalities for indoor supply lines.

Catch basin: An underground grease catchment connected to a drain. Catch basins are commonly bypassed or abandoned.

Cleanout: A removable plug in a trap or a drainpipe that allows easier access to blockages inside.

Closet bend: The elbow-shaped fitting beneath a toilet that carries waste to the main drain.

Codes: See Uniform Plumbing Code.

Compression fitting: A brass or plastic fitting used to join pipe by tightening two nuts that force a ring-like ferrule into the fitting to assure a tight seal.

Coupling: A copper, galvanized steel, plastic, or brass fitting used to connect two lengths of pipe in a straight run.

Dielectric fitting: This fitting joins copper and steel pipe. By means of a specially-designed plastic washer, it insulates the pipes from an otherwise corrosive chemical reaction. See also transition fitting.

Diverter: A valve on a faucet that changes the flow of water from a faucet spout to a hand sprayer or, on a tub/shower faucet, from the tub spout to the shower head.

Drain-waste-vent (DWV) system: The network of pipes and fittings that carries liquid and solid wastes out of a building and to a public sewer, a septic tank, or a cesspool, and allows for the passage of sewer gases to the outside.

Drum trap: Found in older homes, this cylindrical trap is built into the floor and covered with a brass, chrome-plated, or expandable cap.

Elbow: A fitting used to change the direction of a water supply line. Also known as an ell. Bends do the same thing with drain-waste-vent lines.

Fall: A word used to express the slope drain lines are installed at to ensure proper waste drainage. Minimum fall per foot is ¼ inch.

Fitting: Any connector (except a valve) that lets you join pipes of similar or dissimilar size or material in straight runs or at an angle.

Fixture: Any of several devices that provide a supply of water or sanitary disposal of liquid or solid wastes. Tubs, showers, sinks, lavatories, and toilets are examples.

Fixture drain: The drainpipe and trap leading from a fixture to the main drain.

Flux: A stiff jelly brushed or smeared on the surfaces of copper and brass pipes and fittings before joining them to assist in the cleaning and bonding processes.

Hammer arrester: A shock absorbing device that provides a cushion of air to prevent water hammer.

I.D.: The abbreviation for inside diameter. All plumbing pipes are sized according to their inside diameter. See also O.D.

Loop vent: A vent installation for a kitchen island that loops as high as possible under the island and connects to a stack by means of a vent line that runs under the floor.

Main drain: That portion of the drainage system between the fixture drains and the sewer drain. See also fixture drain and sewer drain.

Nipple: A 12-inch or shorter pipe with threads on both ends that is used to join fittings. A close nipple has threads that run from both ends to the center.

No-hub fitting: A neoprene gasket with a stainless-steel band that tightens to join PVC drain pipe to ABS or cast-iron pipe.

Nominal size: The designated dimension of a pipe or fitting. It varies slightly from the actual size.

O.D.: The abbreviation for outside diameter. See also I.D.

PE: Flexible PE (polyethylene) supply pipe is the newest type of plastic pipe. Many codes restrict its use.

PVC: Polyvinyl-chloride (PVC) pipe is the most commonly accepted type of plastic drain pipe. PVC is sometimes also used for supply pipes, but most codes no longer allow it for hot water supply lines because heat causes it to shrink, weakening joints.

Packing: A plastic or metallic cord-like material used chiefly around faucet stems. When compressed it results in a watertight seal.

Pipe joint compound: A material applied to pipe threads to ensure a watertight or airtight seal. Also called pipe dope.

Pipe-thread tape: A synthetic pipe-thread wrapping that seals a joint.

Plumber's putty: A dough-like material used as a sealer. Often a bead of it is placed around the underside of toilets and deck-mount sinks and lavatories.

PSI: The abbreviation for pounds per square inch. Water pressure is rated at so many PSIs.

Reducer: A fitting with different size openings at either end used to go from a larger to a smaller pipe.

Riser: A pipe supplying water to a location or a supply tube running from a pipe to a sink or toilet.

Rough-in: The early stages of a plumbing project during which supply and drain-waste-vent lines are run to their destinations. All work done after the rough-in is finish work.

Run: Any length of pipe or pipes and fittings going in a straight line.

Saddle tee valve: A fitting used to tap into a water line without having to cut the line apart. Some local codes prohibit its use.

Sanitary fitting: Any of several connectors used to join drain-waste-vent lines. Their design helps direct waste downward.

Sanitary sewer: Underground drainage network that carries liquid and solid wastes to a treatment plant.

Septic tank: A reservoir that collects and separates liquid and solid wastes, then digests the organic material and passes the liquid waste onto a drainage field.

Sewer drain: That part of the drainage system that carries liquid and solid wastes from a dwelling to a sanitary sewer, septic tank, or a cesspool.

Soil stack: A vertical drainpipe that carries waste toward the sewer drain. The main soil stack is the largest vertical drain line of a building into which liquid and solid wastes from branch drains flow. See also vent stack.

Stop valve: A device installed in a water supply line, usually near a fixture, that lets you shut off the water supply to one fixture without interrupting service to the rest of the system. Stop valves are built into some tub/shower faucets.

Storm sewer: An underground drainage network designed to collect and carry away water coming into it from storm drains. See also sanitary sewer.

Stubout: A brass drop-ear elbow which has one threaded opening and two holes which can be screwed tightly against a wall. Some can be sweated; some have threaded ends.

Sweating: A technique used to produce watertight joints between copper pipe and fittings. A pipe and fitting are cleaned, coated with flux, and pushed together. When the fitting is heated to the proper temperature with a torch, solder is drawn into the joint by capillary action to make the seal.

Tailpiece: That part of a fixture drain that runs from the drain outlet to the trap.

Tee: A T-shaped fitting used to tap into a length of pipe at a 90-degree angle for the purposes of beginning a branch line.

Transition fitting: Any one of several fittings that joins pipe made of dissimilar materials, such as copper and plastic, plastic and cast iron, or galvanized steel and copper.

Trap: Part of a fixture drain required by code that creates a water seal to prevent sewer gases from penetrating a home's interior.

Uniform Plumbing Code: A nationally recognized set of guidelines prescribing safe plumbing practices. Local codes take precedence over it.

Union: A fitting used in runs of threaded pipe to facilitate disconnecting the line (without ever having to cut it).

Vent: The vertical or sloping horizontal portion of a drain line that permits sewer gases to rise out of the house. Every fixture in a house must be vented.

Vent stack: The upper portion of a vertical drain line through which gases pass directly to the outside. The main vent stack is the portion of the main vertical drain line above the highest fixture connected to it through which sewer gases from various fixtures escape upward and to the outside.

Water hammer: A loud noise caused by a sudden stop in the flow of water, which causes pipes to repeatedly hit up against a nearby framing member.

Water supply system: The network of pipes and fittings that transports water under pressure to fixtures and other water-using equipment and appliances.

Wet wall: A strategically place cavity (usually a 2×6 wall) in which the main drain/vent stack and a cluster of supply and drain-waste-vent lines are housed.

Y: A Y-shaped drainage fitting that serves as the starting point for a branch drain supplying one of more fixtures.

INDEX

METRIC CONVERSIONS

U.S. Units to Metric Equivalents			Metric Units to U.S. Equivalents		
To convert from	Multiply by	To get	To convert from	Multiply by	To get
Inches	25.4	Millimeters	Millimeters	0.0394	Inches
Inches	2.54	Centimeters	Centimeters	0.3937	Inches
Feet	30.48	Centimeters	Centimeters	0.0328	Feet
Feet	0.3048	Meters	Meters	3.2808	Feet
Yards	0.9144	Meters	Meters	1.0936	Yards
Square inches	6.4516	Square centimeters	Square centimeters	0.1550	Square inches
Square feet	0.0929	Square meters	Square meters	10.764	Square feet
Square yards	0.8361	Square meters	Square meters	1.1960	Square yards
Acres	0.4047	Hectares	Hectares	2.4711	Acres
Cubic inches	16.387	Cubic centimeters	Cubic centimeters	0.0610	Cubic inches
Cubic feet	0.0283	Cubic meters	Cubic meters	35.315	Cubic feet
Cubic feet	28.316	Liters	Liters	0.0353	Cubic feet
Cubic yards	0.7646	Cubic meters	Cubic meters	1.308	Cubic yards
Cubic yards	764.55	Liters	Liters	0.0013	Cubic yards

*To convert from degrees Fahrenheit (F) to degrees Celsius (C),
first subtract 32, then multiply by 5/9.*

*To convert from degrees Celsius to degrees Fahrenheit,
multiply by 9/5, then add 32.*